GILGAMESH

GILGAMESH

——— The Life of a Poem ———

MICHAEL SCHMIDT

PRINCETON AND OXFORD

PRINCETON UNIVERSITY PRESS

Published by Princeton University Press

41 William Street, Princeton, New Jersey 08540

6 Oxford Street, Woodstock, Oxfordshire OX20 1TR

press.princeton.edu

LCCN: 2019936031

ISBN: 9780691195247

British Library Cataloging-in-Publication Data is available

Editorial: Ben Tate and Charlie Allen

Production Editorial: Debbie Tegarden

Text Design: C. Alvarez-Gaffin

Jacket Design: Amanda Weiss

Production: Merli Guerra

Publicity: Jodi Price

Copyeditor: Jodi Beder

Jacket Credit: Partially broken tablet V of the
Epic of Gilgamesh. Old Babylonian period, 2003–1595 BCE.
The Sulaymaniyah Museum, Iraq.

This book has been composed in Charis SIL

Printed on acid-free paper. ∞

Printed in the United States of America

1 3 5 7 9 10 8 6 4 2

FOR ANTONY GORMLEY

AND IN MEMORY OF

MICHAEL POWELL,

EXTRAORDINARY LIBRARIAN

AND FRIEND

. . . from 3378 BC (date man's 1st city, name and face of creator also known) in unbroken series first at Uruk, then from the seaport Lagash out into colonies in the Indus Valley and, circa 2500, the Nile, until date 1200 BC or thereabouts, civilization had ONE CENTER, Sumer, in all directions, that this one people held such exact and superior force that all peoples around them were sustained by it, nourished, increased, advanced, that a city was a coherence which, for the first time since the ice, gave man the chance to join knowledge to culture and, with this weapon, shape dignities of economics and value sufficient to make daily life itself a dignity and a sufficiency.

Charles Olson, 'The Gate and the Center', *Collected Prose,* p. 170

Contents

Acknowledgements

I would like to thank those writers who responded to my questions about their relationship with Gilgamesh, many of whom I quote in the book. In particular I am grateful for the care and detailed help of Iain Bamforth, Edward Hsu, Jenny Lewis, Charles Schmidt and Harry Gilonis, who sent me in useful directions. I would also like to raise my hat to my Princeton line editor Jodi Beder: her contributions are warmly appreciated.

To the Master and Fellows of Trinity College, Cambridge, where I enjoyed a Visiting Fellow Commonership in 2017–8, thanks are due, and at Trinity in particular to Professor Angela Leighton and for his patience and kindness to Professor Nicolas Postgate; also in Cambridge to Dr Selena Wisnom and at St John's College to Professor Patrick Boyde. I had the pleasure of hearing and meeting Professor Andrew George during the writing of this book and am entirely in debt to him for his illuminating scholarship and good humour, which I hope will extend to the errors and omissions of this book.

Preface

'So poetry tackles what is not yet, what is lost, what the kestrel is when it is all kestrel.'

R. F. Langley

GILGAMESH is a confusion of stories. There is, first, the broken story told by the poem itself. Then, the story of why the clay tablets it was written on got broken into so many fragments, scattered over a vast area from Turkey to southern Iran, and were lost for millennia. Then, how it was re-discovered, by accident and then by design, in various archaeological digs, the conventional heroisms of Victorian derring-do spurred on by competing expeditions from Germany and France. And how the discoveries continue to this day, sometimes thanks to excavation, other times as the result of museum and archive sackings and antiquity-trafficking, in the wake of wars and anarchy.

The story of the poem's recovery is nothing short of a metonymic account of almost two centuries of Middle Eastern history.

And how exactly were the eleven (or twelve) tablets of the poem reassembled, a jigsaw—actually, several jigsaws in different languages and from periods separated by centuries. The pieces, drawn from dozens of sites, are now scattered through dozens of the world's museums and libraries, in Berlin, Paris, London, Oxford, Chicago, Baghdad . . . the fragments mixed in with tens of thousands of unrelated fragments—inventories, invoices, omen texts, school exercises, letters, laws, laments. . . .

And then, the most heroic story of all, how the complex lost languages in which the poem was written—Old Babylonian, Standard Babylonian,* Hittite and others which ceased to be voiced and written thousands of years ago—were gradually recovered, first the cuneiform script, and then the sounds and sense, a continuing triumph of philological genius and perseverance. *Gilgamesh* even in its damaged present form is an ongoing labour of scholarship and love.

Gilgamesh has become a canonical work. Schoolchildren learn the story. Undergraduates encounter it as an assigned or recommended book. Enkidu, who loves animals, saves them from trappers and hunters, and becomes the best friend a man could have, is a favourite with younger readers, the most popular figure in the story, a talisman for ecologists. The poem leaves so much space for the reader's imagination that when we read it, while we all go on the same narrative journey and reach the same destination, we carry different luggage with us. Your vision of the land around Uruk-the-Sheepfold, of Humbaba's cedar (or pine) forest, of Uta-napishti's boat, of the view of Uruk from the walls, will differ from mine. The netherworld for you and for me will appear quite different.

If we read Homer or Virgil we share much more common ground, in part because Homer describes more, in part because the poems have been so thoroughly assimilated into our literary and artistic culture that we know the characters and scenes even before we read the poems. *Gilgamesh* is sparse by comparison. It is 3200 lines and part-lines long (at present: if ever fully restored

---

* Both Old Babylonian and Standard Babylonian are dialects of Akkadian.

it will run to about 3600 lines) as against 15,693 lines in the *Iliad* and 12,110 in the *Odyssey*, not to mention the 9896 lines of the *Aeneid*. The textures of the Greek poems, and how much more so of the Latin, are worked and re-worked: there is much deliberate poetry in them and little approximation. The *Aeneid* in particular is charged with poetic intent, and we are aware throughout of the presence not only of the poet, whose mastery of prosody and poetic form is unrivalled, but also of his chief reader the emperor Augustus, whom the poem obliquely celebrates. We are also aware of echoes of some of the poems upon which Virgil modelled his.

Gilgamesh is quite another kind of poem. It came together over centuries and is on the face of it less artful than Virgil and Homer. It does not appear to have a specific political or civic target. We are not even clear if it had an audience, or who such an audience might have comprised. In modern terms, it has not had time to sink in, in part at least because it has not yet found its great translator, its George Chapman (Ovid), its John Dryden (Virgil), its Alexander Pope (Homer), its Edward Fitzgerald (Omar Khayyam). Not for lack of trying: there are numerous modern renditions, but *Gilgamesh* is still in waiting. The most convincing contemporary translations are by scholars who insist that their versions acknowledge the gaps and difficulties of the original. Yet it is a poem widely read by contemporary writers, who draw a variety of formal and imaginative energies from it.

• • •

I wrote to fifty poets across the Anglophone world and asked them five questions about *Gilgamesh*. It is hard to frame questions that do not prompt specific answers and reveal more about the questioner than the poem. I wanted the poem to pose its questions.

1. When do you first remember encountering the poem
   and in which translation (or which adaptation and
   medium)? [What mattered was the first remembered
   encounter, the real engagement. It might have come
   not by textual means but via the collages of Anselm
   Kiefer, or a surprising episode of *Star Trek: the Next
   Generation*, or via oratorios, operas or animations.]
2. Which is now your preferred translation or version?
3. Do you recall your initial impression of the poem?
   What residual relationship do you have with it in
   your own writing and thinking about writing? [Men
   and women responded very differently, almost as
   though the material of the poem is fundamentally
   gendered; and unless the reader is able to engage
   with the textures of the language or to historicise
   response, the narrative can alienate anyone impatient
   with heroes and dragons.]
4. Do you place it, in your literal or mental library, on a
   shelf with epics, with scripture, on another shelf
   (which?), or on no shelf at all?
5. Is *Gilgamesh* an informing element in your imaginative
   and critical being, or 'being', and if so, in what ways?

Most respondents first read the poem in N. K. Sandars's prose translation, the original Penguin Classics version. Dick Davis, the poet and major Persian translator, describes it: 'the prose of [her] version is quasi King James Bible English, loosened but recognizably on that model, and I have always been a sucker for prose like this, and this was/is an added reason it has remained my preferred version, even though I am aware that this is a rather dubiously appropriate model.' Some of those reared on Sandars have gone on to other preferences. But there is something to be said for a prose version first time round: it gives the narrative clearly, without the distraction of gaps and fissures. It does, however, pose other problems.

This book recounts some of the stories surrounding *Gilgamesh*. It looks at the work itself and tries to read it without the back-projections that mar so much reading, the belief that 'they' were like an earlier version of 'us', and their concerns were in some way prototypes of ours. The otherness of *Gilgamesh* is what this book tries to be about, though the habits of the age infect the author, who is in the first degree guilty, being—like most of the poem's would-be translators—unable to read the work in any of its original languages.

GILGAMESH

INTRODUCTION

GILGAMESH, the oldest long poem in the world, is a relatively *new* classic. Parts of it were rediscovered, inscribed on clay tablets in cuneiform writing, in Mesopotamia (modern-day Iraq and environs) early in the nineteenth century. Since then it has become a work in progress, a collaboration led by Assyriologists, their discipline born of the poem itself, joined by archaeologists, ruin raiders, jihadis, museum curators, philologists, scholars, and writers who feel entitled to the poem even when they lack the linguistic means to look it directly in the face.

Gilgamesh: is it the first road novel,* the first trip to hell, the first Deluge, the first heterosexual romance in poetry? Does the love that dare not speak its name very nearly speak its name here for the first time? The poet Rod Mengham reflects, 'I love the fact that the earliest literary text we have enshrines friendship as the bedrock of our negotiations with the world and time.' *Gilgamesh* also gives the first account of the uneasy triumph of nurture over nature.

Its composition began more than two millennia BCE and ended around 700 BCE. It prefigures almost every literary tone and trope and suggests all the genres, from dramatic to epic, from lament to lyric and chronicle, that have followed it. It is political, it is religious. Its fractures foreshadow Modernism, which it teased and nourished, teases and nourishes. It is a whole

---

* Gregory Corso called Gilgamesh 'proto-Jack Kerouac' and Enkidu 'proto-Neal Cassady'.

synthesized from fragments. Breakage is part of what and how it now means.

Most poems invite interpretation. *Gilgamesh* invites, indeed requires, construction. Modern readers have to participate, select, invent. It does not let them rest. The more informed readers are, the more similar—we might expect—their readings will be. Yet, though the overarching narratives that scholars trace are broadly similar, their translations, setting out from the same tablets, differ so substantially in interpretation that readers might feel they are approaching quite different poems.

The occasions, subjects and themes of the poem, especially the protagonist's longing to avoid death, are folded into the formal accidents that surround its survival. Because of how it was written down, time and the elements contributed to it as to no other poem. It spent millennia buried. Unearthed, it wears marks of weather, excavation tools, human delinquency and restoration. It shows its age and celebrates its material presence, a partial survival.

But we will never penetrate to the subjectivity of the poem, the 'I' of the narrator. Indeed, as with the authorial persona we call Homer, the 'I' does not exist *in* the poem, and if translators provide a stable narrator, it will be an invention of theirs rather than a presence in the actual text. Much more than the Homeric poems, *Gilgamesh* is provisional, and not—and never—a finished site refined by interpretation.

The growing text of *Gilgamesh* is an increasingly plausible approximation of an original, based on damaged Standard Babylonian tablets. It is re-made with materials drawn from different millennia and languages, a kind of cento—that species of poetic composition assembled from other related works, trying to make a new whole. Because of discoveries and re-interpretations of older tablets, the words won't settle. They change before our eyes; the poem remains provisional, shifting like dunes.

As non-specialists, we find meaning as we read, or read in, the poem. We help to produce it by acts of selection, emphasis and omission. Given the unstable text, we're always on shaky ground. No other literary adventure demands quite so much risk and care, so great an investment from the reader, as *Gilgamesh* does. Few poems provide such uncertain yet sometimes exhilarating rewards. Reading is a matter of tuning and retuning. Given the damaged state of the tablets and the ambiguities of the languages in which it survives, we can never tune in to the poem precisely; there is static and the volume refuses to be evenly controlled. There are no rests, only gaps: a series of narrative highlights, equally weighted, though the tempo and dynamics change from episode to episode. With the passage of poem time, because *Gilgamesh* traces a history, the action (which begins with the protagonist as an oversexed youth in Uruk and ends with him bereaved, exhausted, accepting his own mortality, and still king, in the same city) slows in pace, the sky goes dark.

Gilgamesh, like Odysseus and Aeneas, is a protagonist in process, and he achieves repose only at the very end. We have to stay alert at all times. When we look for an author we see that *Gilgamesh* is made by a river, by fire, by generations of scribes, by shepherds, ruin-robbers, archaeologists and scholars. In all the debris there are literally no vestiges of an identifiable poet to be found. (We will come to the question of the redactor Sin-leqi-unninni in due course.)

The early Old Babylonian stories had a *use* of some sort. The most obvious use we can imagine for them is as entertainments, but entertainments in a religious, ceremonial, or a civic context, contributing to other activities and not ends in themselves. All the same, these episodes are 'stand-alones', not chapters in a larger work. Some have a felt religious, though hardly a spiritual, dimension, and as writing, as written, they belong to the scribal and priestly classes. What the speakers of Standard Babylonian made, when they joined up stories that were already ancient in their day, was different, and what remains of that amalgamated whole is the poem this book is about.

When the *Gilgamesh* texts began to be translated into English, their literary impact was slow and decisive. Into a canon based in the Bible and the Greek and Latin classics, a religious and a secular canon with a highly developed culture of reception and interpretation grown up around it, entered a new text that belonged, as it were, in both currents and in neither. It was millennia older than either, with elements in common with each, which unsettled our understanding and gave us a sense of the extending, shadowy backstories of our traditions.

Most literary translators fill in *Gilgamesh*'s blanks and resolve its riddles, trying to free us to be contented literary consumers, untroubled by the distracting questions that it raises: questions of a semantic nature and also of theme, content and the mechanics of transmission. The most popular translations, those of Sandars, already mentioned, and of Stephen Mitchell, neither of whom had direct access to the original languages, stand guilty as charged. The translations that stay closest to the Standard Babylonian text, Benjamin R. Foster's, Stephanie Dalley's, and, particularly, Andrew George's evolving translation, are the best to build our reading on. The creative realisation in their versions devolves in large part on us, non-specialist readers. We are made brave by the editorial generosity of these Assyriologists and of their colleagues working in this busy field.

RIDDLES

ON 21 November 2017, when I was so engrossed in reading for this book that everything seemed to point to *Gilgamesh*, BBC Radio 4 announced the 'Puzzle for Today'. Dr Steve Humble, Head of Education at Newcastle University, called his teaser 'The Giant Monster Puzzle':

A Giant's head is sixty centimeters long and its legs are as long as its head and three-quarters of the body. If its body is a third of its whole length, how big is the Giant?

This put me in mind of a recently translated cuneiform tablet with previously unknown lines from *Gilgamesh*, in which the king's dimensions are defined. Andrew George translates it.

Eleven cubits was his height,
Four cubits his chest, from nipple to nipple.
A triple cubit his feet and a rod his stride,
A triple cubit the beard of his cheek . . .

Gilgamesh ruled the ancient city of Uruk, one of the earliest settlements that can genuinely be called a city in scale and importance. Being 'two-thirds god and one third man,' he is huge, as befits so primordial a figure. The novelist Ali Smith, reviewing Edwin Morgan's dramatisation, characterises the poem as '4,000-year-old *Gilgamesh*, a story whose subject is immortality, whose voice is resoundingly anonymous and whose terms are resolutely human.' Even despite its age, there is nothing primitive about it. It is a work of sophistication, especially in the subtlety of its language, which suggests that in its prehistory there are even ancienter works on which it drew.

Ever since George Smith published his sensational 'The Chaldean Account of the Deluge',* the Gilgamesh Flood story, the poem's restoration has seemed a priority among biblical scholars. Smith originally reported:

> A short time back I discovered among the Assyrian tablets in the British Museum, an account of the flood [. . .] For convenience of working, I had divided the collection of Assyrian tablets [. . .] into sections, according to the subject matter of the inscriptions. I have recently been examining the division comprising the Mythological and Mythical tablets, and from this section I obtained a number of tablets, giving a curious series of legends and including a copy of the story of the Flood. On discovering these documents, which were much mutilated, I searched over all the collections of fragments of inscriptions, consisting of several thousands of smaller pieces, and ultimately recovered 80 fragments of these legends; by the aid of which I was enabled to restore nearly all the text of the description of the Flood, and considerable portions of the other legends. These tablets were originally at least twelve in number, forming one story or set of legends, the account of the Flood being on the eleventh tablet. Of the inscription describing the Flood, there are fragments of three copies containing the same texts; these copies belong to the time of Assurbanipal, or about 660 years before the Christian era, and they were found in the library of that monarch in the palace at

* *Transactions of the Society of Biblical Archaeology* 2 [1873]:213–34.

Nineveh. The original text, according to the statements on the tablets, must have belonged to the city of Erech [Uruk], and it appears to have been either written in, or translated into the Semitic Babylonian, at a very early period.

The discovery of an account of a universal Deluge prior to the story of Noah, but possibly related to it either as a source or analogue, was front-page news in Europe and the United States. Newspaper sponsorship precipitated further exploration. Every time a new piece of *Gilgamesh* turns up, even today when the tide of faith has ebbed, the news finds its way into the papers. *Gilgamesh* has proven, since its resurrection began, what Ezra Pound declared a good poem should be, 'news that stays news', though he had a different sense of 'news' in mind.

Paradoxically, Gilgamesh's over-riding desire to live forever, which drives him to the very ends of the earth to meet Noah's *semblable*, is responsible for funding the development of the discipline that came to be known as Assyriology. With his wife beside him, Uta-napishti (whose name means 'I found life'), the proto-Noah (whose name means 'rest' or 'comfort') tells Gilgamesh a story at once strange and strangely familiar.

• • •

Returning to the 'new' measurements of King Gilgamesh: 'Eleven cubits was his height,' we are told. If a cubit runs from the elbow to the tip of the middle finger, between 48 and 56 centimeters, then Gilgamesh, more than semi-divine, is quite tall, between five and six metres; and though we are not told the scale of the mere human inhabitants of Uruk, his subjects, we can imagine that they are much smaller than he is, so that when he wrestles with them at the start of the poem they do not provide much of a challenge. We might suggest, erring on the generous side, that they were on average three cubits tall, between a quarter and a third his height. The passage continues:

> Four cubits his chest, from nipple to nipple.
> A triple cubit his feet and a rod his stride,
> A triple cubit the beard of his cheek . . .

From height to nipple to nipple to foot to beard . . . the observing eye—not a narrator's—flutters over the king's body, measuring it, but in no particular order. For the modern reader, the surprise of his relative scale is overtaken by a sense of incongruity in his proportions. He is over a third as broad as he is tall. And how huge his feet, and how excessive, though doubtless tightly curled, the beard on his cheek. He sounds the sort of figure we might meet in comic books or manga, unless his dimensions are intended to evoke not his actual physical scale or what he looks like but something qualitative about him. We measure him not to visualise him but to get a different sense of him.

The American scholar and translator Benjamin R. Foster declares,

> We Assyriologists have a serene feeling of expectancy that scholars of other ancient dead literatures cannot realistically allow themselves: more ancient manuscripts will surface of our favorite compositions, as well as of works we didn't even know existed. Therefore translations of Babylonian literature need constant updating, expansion, and refinement.

This 'serene feeling of expectancy' attaches to the uncertainties of scholarship as well. Point out to the great Assyriologist Andrew George that the dimensions of Gilgamesh in the new fragment are, in terms of bodily proportion, ridiculous, unless

Gilgamesh is a relation of Obelix, and he calmly remarks, 'Yes, there's something wrong with it. It needs more work.' This provisionality, accepting that the existing text (or our understanding of it) will be improved, is tonic to the puzzled reader. George adds meditatively that in three or four hundred years people will look back at the early generations of *Gilgamesh* scholarship (we are now into the seventh or eighth) with wry good humour at their errors, their optimism, their naivety, relative to what will then be known. There have been a hundred generations of Virgil scholarship and a hundred and fifty of Homer. Though our poem predates Homer's by over a millennium, and the principal languages in which it was composed, Old Babylonian and Standard Babylonian, are far deader than ancient Greek, with no modern linguistic progeny, *Gilgamesh* is still the new kid on the scholarly block.

King Gilgamesh's dimensions provide a riddle more complicated than the 'Giant Monster Puzzle' because, if we are literal-minded (and what else can we be when we are being given specific measurements?), they strain credulity. We accept giants readily enough, but if we are told a giant is also a paragon, we tend to resist distortion. The solution to the Gilgamesh puzzle cannot be expressed straightforwardly as two metres and eighty-eight centimeters. The BBC monster is not even half the height of our king. And Professor Humble did not measure his Giant's chest from nipple to nipple, his feet, or his beard.

. . .

All through the poem numbers are used in ways that feel more emblematic than literal. Cuneiform writing was first invented to make inventories and record business transactions, and we should not be surprised to find lists in *Gilgamesh*. But in this and other poetry texts, specific numbers are associated with ritual, magic, symbolism or plain tradition. They are used less to enumerate (after all, what does it matter if it takes three or eight days to make a trip?—you don't measure in miles but in elapsed time) than to conform the narrative to an underlying or a transcendent pattern. The number three occurs frequently: cycles of three dreams, three blows to bring down the monster Humbaba, three snorts from the Bull of Heaven, and so on. Returns from long journeys seem to take three days. Six-and-seven also recurs: Enkidu's first scene of priapic love-making lasts six days and seven nights; in the ark there are six levels and seven decks; the sleep-challenge to Gilgamesh (which he fails) lasts six days and seven nights.

After three, seven by itself is the most commonly repeated number. Enkidu downs seven jugs of beer, the monster Humbaba has seven auras, the city gates have seven bolts, seven mountain chains are crossed to get to the cedar forest, lamentation lasts seven days and nights. The seven judges of hell make lightning at the Deluge, seven sages laid the foundations of Uruk, seven and then another seven cauldrons of incense are lighted after the Deluge to entice the gods, and so on. When the poem enters into patterns of repetition, threes and sevens are the charm numbers.

Gilgamesh has a literal aspect. It tells some stories which connect at various levels. But underpinning the story are further patterns that we sometimes infer, sometimes sense. Other times they call attention to themselves and seem to distort the narrative, until something comes along—a new tablet, a new interpretation—which makes sense of them.

If we take the poem broken tablet by broken tablet, we can see what patterns of narrative and design emerge.

TWO ROADS DIVERGE

THERE are two incipits (beginnings) to *Gilgamesh*. The Old Babylonian, with surviving tablets from around the eighteenth century BCE (probably based on earlier tablets which have yet to come to light), leads into a *Gilgamesh* story but not into the big poem itself. It spotlights the young king in his larger-than-life tyranny and glory: *Shūtur eli sharrī*, 'Surpassing all other kings, heroic in stature, / brave scion of Uruk, wild bull on the rampage!' Immediately we are introduced to his vices, his insistence on fighting, his anti-social habit of exercising first-night rights with the brides-to-be of his subjects. He is soon made to live up to the last epithet, 'wild bull on the rampage'. There is no narrator: the story utters itself.

In the later version, *Shūtur eli sharrī* is shunted thirty lines into the poem. The Standard Babylonian poem, from between 1400 and 1100 BCE, reworks the older material. The stories, discrete adventures starring Gilgamesh, draw moral lessons from things he does. *Gilgamesh* joins these stories into a single, if not quite a continuous, poem. Some of the joins are awkward. The new incipit is *Sa naqba imuru* or *ša nagbu imuru,* and the text survives in two manuscript tablet traditions. The older versions are mainly from Assurbanipal's library in Nineveh (Kuyunjik); the later versions are fifth century BCE, from the libraries of Uruk and Babylon itself.

The Standard Babylonian *Gilgamesh* is more formal, more sombre in its opening, than the separate stories might have led us to expect, as if the king and the poem were already older and wiser, and the body of the poem, the adventures, are flashbacks, though they are not presented as such. Andrew George's 1999 translation, mainly into quatrains with some formal variation (my preferred version), stays as close as his English can to the surviving originals. It opens:

> He who saw the Deep, the country's foundation,
>> [who] knew . . . , was wise in all matters!
> [Gilgamesh, who] saw the Deep, the country's foundation
>> [who] knew . . . , was wise in all matters!
>
> [He] . . . everywhere . . .
>> and [*learnt*] of everything the sum of wisdom.
> He saw what was secret, discovered what was hidden,
>> he brought back a tale of before the Deluge.

What did he know? What, we did not know, waiting as we were for further fragments to come to light, to fill out the picture. And then in 2006 the pieces fell into place with a new tablet discovery.

> He who saw the Deep, the country's foundation,
>> who knew the proper ways, was wise in everything!
> Gilgamesh, who saw the Deep, the country's foundation,
>> who knew the proper ways, was wise in everything!
>
> He everywhere explored the seats of power,
>> knew of everything the sum of wisdom.
> He saw what was secret, discovered what was hidden,
>> brought back a tale of before the Deluge.

In George's first text above, translated from Standard Babylonian sources, we could trust words in roman type; and we could be quite confident about words supplied in square brackets because the translator inferred them from context or from usage elsewhere in this, or in other Standard Babylonian texts. There is abundant verbatim repetition that helps with half-erased lines. What is in italics in square brackets seems to him plausible interpolation, but is not authorised by any existing fragment or parallel. And the ellipses are precisely that, breaks that cannot confidently be repaired. How close his suppositions came to what the 2006 tablet yields! Our resilient, patchwork Gilgamesh, part historical, part mythical, peers over the walls of Uruk not at us, exactly, but in our general direction, because, although Gilgamesh cannot see us, we—ghostlike, insubstantial, architects of vain towers—people his afterlife. We are recognised by the poem and addressed directly, collectively, when he commands us to 'See' in the fifth line below.* Restoration continues,

He came a far road, was weary but at peace;
    all his labours were set on a tablet of stone.
He had the rampart built of Uruk-the-Sheepfold,
    of holy Eanna, the sacred storehouse.

See its wall like a strand of wool,
    View its parapet that none could copy!
Take the stairway of a bygone era,
    draw near to Eanna, seat of Ishtar the goddess,
that no later king could ever copy!

---

* When these lines recur at the end of the poem, the 'See' or 'Survey' is no longer addressed to an assumed 'us' but to Gilgamesh's then companion Ur-shanabi.

Climb Uruk's wall and walk back and forth!
　Survey its foundations, examine the brickwork!
Were its bricks not fired in an oven?
　Did the Seven Sages not lay its foundations?

For a moment the poem goes into prose, a modulation ensuring that no poetic ambiguity will affect the measuring out of the city.

[A square mile is] city, [a square mile] date-grove, a square mile is clay-pit, half a square mile the temple of Ishtar: [three square miles] and a half is Uruk's expanse.

Open the tablet-box of cedar,
release its clasp of bronze!

[Lift] the lid of its secret,
　pick up the tablet of lapis lazuli and read out—
the travails of Gilgamesh, all that he went through.

George conveys a strong sense of scale, but the only actual *image* we are given, the single specific detail, is the cedar box (is the cedar from the Humbaba expedition, we wonder, when we read the poem a second time) whose clasp we release, whose lid we raise, exposing and taking out the precious secret it has kept.

This can stand as a metaphor for our challenge as readers. We have been given access, collaborating with the scholar-translator, to the process of putting the poem back together again. So many pieces are missing. . . . George does not let us relax: his quest is our quest and we are kept on our toes as we would be by a series of riddles. Every line raises semantic and interpretational problems. We need only set Foster's version beside George's to see how many choices are involved, not only in the matter of translation but in the prosody and layout of the English version. Foster says:

> He who saw the wellspring, the foundations of the land,
>   Who knew [. . .], was wise in all things,
> Gilgamesh, who knew the wellspring, the foundations of
>   the land,
> Who knew [. . .], was wise in all things,
> [He . . .] throughout,
> Full understanding of it all he gained,
> He saw what was secret and revealed what was hidden,
> He brought back tidings from before the flood.

This translation grows from the same roots as George's, but the leaves look very different. Thus George's

> See its wall like a strand of wool,
>   View its parapet that none could copy!

becomes, in Foster,

> See its upper wall, whose facing gleams like copper,
> Gaze at the lower course, which nothing will equal . . .

Two leading scholars diverge: how much work a reader needs to do to infer the form and sense of the undisclosing (or over-ambiguous) original! Part of the problem for translator as for reader is that so little of the poem's context survives, and reading the broken texts we have can entail, apart from imaginative restoration, also imagining the contingencies in which it was first produced and then developed across the dead languages in which it has survived. We are not finished with the strand of wool or the copper gleam quite yet.

. . .

As a reader of *Gilgamesh*, I too had two incipits or starting points. First, in a religious studies class at school we were presented with the *Gilgamesh* Deluge. The Deluge passage remains the poem's most effective calling card. Without it, Assyriology would have developed less rapidly in the nineteenth century than it did. The churches had a vested interest in the Bible proofs that the poem seemed to offer, and newspapers helped fund further exploration: the media in hot pursuit of millennium-old news. My classmates and I read the Deluge more as a document that fed into Bible studies than as part of a poem.

As undergraduates, friends and I read the whole of *Gilgamesh* out of a secular and (we were trying to be poets) formal curiosity. None of us studied the original languages, and we were unaware that N. K. Sandars, our *Gilgamesh* translator of choice, had herself forced the poem into an incompatible classical shape, 'improving' it and adjusting it to an alien genre. She had also worked it into prose. Once we had read it, we found traces of it in the modern poetry we were trying to enjoy, in Charles Olson and Louis Zukofsky, in Basil Bunting and elsewhere. Here was a *modern* modernist resource. Sandars's *The Epic of Gilgamesh* piqued our formal curiosity, but, as we would later see, we were short-changed.

Dick Davis wrote to me describing the impact *Gilgamesh* had when he read it at nineteen. 'For me it's simply the oldest tale still available to us; it's neither scripture nor epic, but something more bed-rock and preceding both. It was an early demonstration to me that early versions of what we are are still in some sense "true".' He remembers the Roman historian Sallust's definition of myth, 'These things have never happened but are always true.' *Gilgamesh* made him

fascinated with oldest tales, and thus with epic, perhaps culminating in my translation of the Persian epic, Ferdowsi's *Shahnameh*, parts of which clearly draw on shadowy survivals of very ancient and probably pre-metal, neolithic, story-telling, that are perhaps, in their earliest iterations, as old as Gilgamesh, and as psychically, and barely paraphrasably, resonant for us.

Gilgamesh impacts on many English-speaking writers. Davis is an English poet with an unusual mastery of traditional forms. Modernists and their heirs have also been affected, though they respond, in the free, fractured, or elliptical forms they devise, to the broken surfaces of the texts. The possibility of the fragment as a sufficient formal unit, the principles of juxtaposition that they learned from this as from venerable Eastern poetic sources, produced a concision that could be accommodated into larger, looser forms. An in-the-end unrestrictive restriction.

The poet Harry Gilonis remembers the early fascination of the fragment and, writing to me, recalls Friedrich Schlegel's observations, 'Many works of the ancients have become fragments. Many works of the moderns are fragments at the time of their origin'; and, 'A fragment is a thought that is determined by itself and determines itself', which, Gilonis comments, 'out-Hegels Hegel'. He understands the dynamic of the 'fragment' and how it can be falsified.

Having looked at scholarly editions of this sort of material, albeit cursorily, I was annoyed beyond the point of being able to take the stuff seriously by Armand Schwerner's *The*

Tablets. I *wanted* to like them—George Oppen's enthusiasm was a powerful vote of confidence—but Schwerner's messy (and un-necessary) re-invention of the *apparatus criticus*—specifically '++++' for missing sections, and the way that he so evidently inserted these gaps for *literary* reasons, rather than making any plausible attempt to imitate the way accidents actually happened to the tablets, all too evident in 'proper' cuneiform editions—irritated me so thoroughly that I couldn't get past it:

turn, turn, turn in the turning, for the time is short
and there is no longer any leisure
for further [mechanic] wanderings
we should always live in the dark empty sky
+++++++++++++++++lightning+++++++++
. . . .
. . . . +++++++++
. . . . red iron and blue sea-urchins from generative slime
and all as unreal as you
the self binding cry of mineral keeps red iron tight
together

Some writers adopted the fragmentation of *Gilgamesh* as a device in their own work to draw readers into the creative process, not so much inviting as compelling them to participate, to provide the necessary jumps between verbal synapses. For others *Gilgamesh* represented a pre-Greco-Roman option, free of long-established cultural traditions, a *new* anciency, an untrammelled resource. Poet and essayist Peter Davidson writes, 'Something that has come to preoccupy me in later life is the "search for an alternative antiquity".' This is more an antecedent than an alternative.

For the English-language Israeli poet Gabriel Levin, *Gilgamesh* is nothing less than 'the originary, Ur-poem and prototype of ancient wisdom literature written in the form of an unending quest for self-knowledge'. It has been a living poetic resource and source for him. In his collection of poems *Ostraca* (1999) he included 'Reading Gilgamesh', a layering of pasts that comes alive in the present of a garden, the figure of Enkidu ('everyone's second self'), and a child, his daughter. 'I imagine my own mock-quest,' he says, describing the poem, 'my own "setting out and return" while spading and hoeing in my back yard and eventually dozing off with my volume of the *Epic* slipping to the ground.'

Now remember the taming
    of Enkidu, how the wild game
    bolted into the bush
        after he lay with love
    and was satisfied;
he who'd sport with gazelles
    and quenched his thirst in their waterholes
was alone and bound in his thoughts
    to the nameless child of pleasure.

Desire confined to the gazing,
    tender ball. Push on,
        urges the month-by-month
    gardener's manual, as if
the yard were the only vantage ground
    from which to sound

> the setting out and return,
>   tacit as the trail
> of the field slug turning a leaf
>   omnivorous (where the dogrose cleaves
> to the cypress).

>   Push on in April
> with the spading and hoeing
>   and consider Enkidu, natural man,
>   everyone's second self,
>   or pet demoniac,
> brainpan teeming with word-stems,
>   as though the bold figure of companionship
> were carved on the transom of every door.

> Nodding to sleep in the noon sun
>   that springs the dragonfly
>   free from its larva; Shams, Shemesh,
>   Shamash the Protector.
>   *Heed the child*
> *that holds your hand.* The right words
>   prised out of the mouth of what
> strange being? The slender volume
>   unclasped slips to the ground.

'Reading Gilgamesh' bears an unsettling resemblance to Seamus Heaney's poem 'Digging', and yet the pasts it mines are deeper than Heaney's: there is no space for atavism in a poem that drives so deeply into the roots of all our common languages and poetries.

• • •

From my undergraduate reading, only Enkidu stayed in memory. It is Enkidu who caused me to accept the invitation to write this little essay on *Gilgamesh*. He is the poem's engaging player, a nearly rounded 'character', most human-seeming despite his unnatural birth, shaped out of clay like a writing tablet; and the most fundamentally transformed by his adventures with animals, with a woman, a man, a monster, with the gods, and then with the prospect of death, and (spoiler alert) death itself. His death is the core of the poem. Modern readers most readily tune into the poem through it. He rages, rages, and then he accepts the dying of the light, his human fate. After he dies *Gilgamesh* moves beyond adventure into lamentation and, finally, finds quite another key.

Sandars's translation has had an incalculable effect on the English sense of the poem. The publisher Allen Lane, who established with his cunning commercial-cultural instinct the Penguin Classics, commissioned it. It was published in 1960. Sandars provided a limited editorial and critical apparatus—a long introduction, a glossary of proper names at the end, and the eleven or twelve tablets of the 'original' divided into seven chapters. She called it *The Epic of Gilgamesh*.

Sandars was an archaeologist. She did not know Old Babylonian or Standard Babylonian. Her version begins not 'He' but 'I'. Introducing a narrator brings the poem in line with later epics, Homer's and Virgil's in particular. This strategy helped reassure readers that *Gilgamesh* was indeed an epic. It was only the first of her many familiarising techniques. Taken together, these techniques make the poem immediate and readable, but they detach it from what it is as revealed in the scholarly versions that reflect the original as we now have it. Sandars's version raises the curtain in a bold fashion:

I will proclaim to the world the deeds of Gilgamesh. This
was the man to whom all things were known; this was the
king who knew the countries of the world. He was wise, he
saw mysteries and knew secret things, be brought to us a
tale of the days before the flood.

Line units are lost in the flow of cadenced prose; the sense of
paired lines, the second a poetic consequence of the first (which
Andrew George imitates in his quatrains, with the second and
fourth lines indented) is forfeited; the gaps that indicate missing
material are papered over. The many repetitions of phrase and
of longer passages, where narrative is reiterated verbatim, are
omitted, made into variations or minimised. Every decision San-
dars takes is in the interests of readability: what matters is what
the poem says, rather than how it says it—as though its formal
properties were not themselves integral to the sense it makes.

One cannot deny the immediacy, indeed the beauty, of Nancy
Sandars's translation, which possesses, not inappropriately given
the presence of so many familiar and unknown gods, the reso-
nance of scripture. It has sold in excess of a million copies, and
it keeps finding new readers. Yet it is remote from the originals
we have, and from the modern translations that grow from them.
In a cavalier, an inadvertently colonial spirit, Sandars's transla-
tion rejects the possibilities of the poem's suggestive *otherness*.
She was a scholar in other fields. She was a lucid writer here.

Allen Lane himself was not into Assyriology. His advisers, like
Sandars herself, were classically trained and steeped in European
languages. He allowed Sandars licence to alter the poem's end-
ing, which she did to dramatic effect. So popular is her version
that most readers today think Gilgamesh dies (with a degree of
pathos and elegance) at the end of the poem. He does not.

Sandars has joined up ill-matched bits of the jigsaw. Andrew George explains, 'As works of literature, the Babylonian poem of *Gilgamesh* and the Old Babylonian poem of the *Death of Bilgames* [Gilgamesh] are entirely separate compositions, in different languages and with different agendas. Together they exhibit an "essential unity" in no greater wise than would a combined *Iliad* and *Aeneid*.' Sandars married the two.

The liberties she took are not permissible today. She puts the protagonist to death, and gives him a solemn funeral. Her prose persuades, the images she invents for the occasions are plainly sacramental. 'Gilgamesh, the son of Ninsun, lies in the tomb,' she writes. 'At the place of offerings he weighed the bread-offering, at the place of libation he poured out the wine.' She brings the narrative to a familiar harbour, but leaves the original at sea. Readers, having enjoyed Sandars (it is hard not to), should promptly move on to one of the scholarly versions.

The most compelling of these is by Andrew George, Professor of Babylonian at the School of Oriental and African Studies (SOAS) in London, who has already been cited *passim*. His version, in the judgement of the American poet Maureen McLane, wins 'HANDS DOWN' (her caps). Many poet-readers agree with her. George proceeds line by line, transcribing, comparing and collating ancient tablets and establishing the soundest texts and, in the 2003 version, transliterating the cuneiform so the poetry is almost audible, and translating it (and later re-translating it) into plain, slightly archaising English. He does not claim to be a poet and so, unpretentiously, achieves remarkable effects without strain, keeping his eye on the original. When in Tablet 10 Gilgamesh tells Uta-napishti how he mourned for Enkidu, he builds his narrative lament to a climax in which the corruption of the flesh is emblematised:

'[Six days] I wept for him [and seven nights:]
   [I did not surrender his body for] burial
   [until a maggot dropped from] his [nostril.]
      [Then I was afraid *that I too would die,*]
   [I grew] fearful of death, [and so wander the] wild.

'What became of [my friend *was too much*] to [bear,]
   so on a far road [I wander the] wild;
what became of my friend Enkidu [*was too much* to bear,]
   so on a far path [I wander the wild].'

We read the translator reading, and he works as a revising poet might, picking up on repetitions, but not prettifying or filling cracks: carefully indicating what isn't there. His reading is believable because it acknowledges, at every bracket, italics and ellipsis, what is, what is suppositious, and what is imaginatively supplied. George's minute negotiation with the material is a triumph of tact. As readers we seem to engage in the very process of restoration.

When he is considering the work of previous editors, George's notes on their questionable readings are generous: he understands why they have made certain decisions and choices, certain inferences, how it is that they have gone their own way. In 'The Application of Thought to Textual Criticism', the most austere of classical scholars, the poet A. E. Housman, wrote, 'Textual criticism is a science, and, since it comprises recension and emendation, it is also an art. It is the science of discovering error in texts and the art of removing it.' For the Assyriologist the peril of error is everywhere. In the first place, the surviving texts are broken; fragments are held in different libraries around the world. Then there is the issue of the original scribal quality of the tablet: was it an apprentice scribe's exercise or a fair copy?

Then come the transitions between and within languages, creating such ambiguities that it is not entirely clear whether, for example, a *balag* or *balagu* is a drum or a lyre. Not every seeming error is an error, and what appears to be commonsensical can be quite wrong. Also, if there are two or more possible meanings, it may be that the ambiguity is intended and a solution has to be found that preserves it.

·   ·   ·

Most *Gilgamesh* translations with poetic pretensions—those published since the Second World War—are 'versions' with scholarly authority as thin as Sandars's own. The American poet Charles Olson, among the most ambitious writers in pursuit of epic in the twentieth century, turned to *Gilgamesh* as to a portent. He writes in 'The Gate and the Center' (1951):

> As I read it, it is an incredibly accurate myth of what happens to the best of men when they lose touch with the primordial and phallic energies and methodologies which, said this predecessor people of ours [the Sumerians or Old Babylonians], make it possible for man, that participant thing, to take up, straight, nature's, live nature's force.

To read the figure of Gilgamesh as 'the best of men' is wilful. For Olson the poem is strictly gendered not only in its *dramatis personae* but in its themes. It is a powerful resource, usefully 'archaic', as he sees it, in a post-modern context. Writing to a friend in 1960, Olson expressed more than a desire, an *intention* to translate 'the Gilgamesh and Inanna stories' which 'should be as familiar as those of the Odyssey'. He is specific: 'I have this in mind: with the *Maximus Poems* at the stage they are, I am able to propose, for the next few months, a job I have wanted to do and have been preparing myself to do for some years, to insert into our own tradition the two poems.' His poem 'Tomorrow' (1941) begins, 'I am Gilgamesh'. (His wonderful short book on *Moby-Dick* takes its title from the novel's first line, 'Call me Ishmael': he had a habit of close identification with his preferred protagonists.) From *Maximus* we can imagine how complex and effective a job he might have made of a translation, and all without reference (given the date, 1941) to N. K. Sandars or, contrariwise,* to Andrew George.

Jenny Lewis's *Gilgamesh Retold: A Response to the Ancient Epic* (2018) is only the second complete English version (after Maureen Gallery Kovacs's of 1989) by a woman poet told in modern poetry. As a response, and a specifically gendered response at that, it stands apart from Stephen Mitchell's and David Ferry's 'retellings'. (The British poet Drew Milne read David Ferry's translation and remembers it as 'quite lively and readable, though more like a tourist guide than an encounter with ancient text'.) Lewis divides the poem into fifteen 'chapters', with a 'Prologue' and an 'Epilogue'. She gives Enkidu rather more agency than earlier translators and she keeps him alive longer than the original warrants, adjusting the poem's proportions. Her formal choices are various. She begins with a gapped or sprung phrasal line:

Gilgamesh knew   he understood   how the waters broke
how the world   was birthed   the weight of life
heavy as a flood   the full womb   the still grave

The imagery of breaking waters, birthing and womb wrest the poem from its usual male-gendered specificity.

---

* '. . . if it was so, it might be; and if it were so, it would be; but as it isn't, it ain't. That's logic.'

Lewis moves into a different form, quatrains, in her second chapter, deploying lines with a marked caesura and two or three stresses on each side of the dividing bar, a prosodically appropriate experiment. Here the women pray to Aruru, and she gives Enkidu human shape. The translator and, with her, the reader clearly find Enkidu irresistible, especially after the violence of Gilgamesh's temper earlier in the 'chapter'. Working from George in particular, she has disregarded many of the textual issues of the original. She suggests fragmentation visually, but resolves it in terms of sense and syntax, the unfolding of metaphor, the magnificence of the emerging man who will be Enkidu:

At last they called | the goddess Aruru
Fertile womb-goddess | who made the first humans
She made life spurt | from the mud of the river
She made life spring | from the clay of the uplands.

The great Aruru | knew the right answer—
To fashion a man | equal to Gilgamesh
An untamed man | to tame the tyrant
An untaught man | to teach him secrets.

Out of the silence | out of the sunlight
Out of the shadows | that carpet the forest
Stepped a man, beautiful | strong like an eagle
Stepped a man, god-like | lithe as a lion.

His hair rolled down | like waves of a torrent
His beard luxuriant | bushy as barley
Dense and waving | the hair of his body
Like an animal god | he stood in the forest.

This approach, relating the form chosen for the chapter to the changes of theme and tone (she goes on into blank verse, free verse, 'scatter' verse, prose), makes the poem speak in different ways from versions that have come before. It is the kind of translation Shiduri the tavern-keeper in Tablet 10 would have admired. It might persuade a reader like the British poet Carol Rumens, who declared, 'I'd only read [Gilgamesh] again if a woman poet translated it, and, in doing so, radically "critiqued" it', to reassess her own response to Gilgamesh, which was hardened by the Mitchell experience.

When the British poet laureate Ted Hughes died, he had on his 'to do' list a dramatic adaptation of Gilgamesh for the Young Vic theatre in London. He mapped it out in six parts, subdivided into acts and scenes. He insisted that despite the poem's mythic scale and scope, the protagonists were like classical and modern dramatic characters, imbued with an inner life, even at moments when they appear to transcend the human scale. Properly realized, he thought the poem might speak to the present day as a kind of archetypal experience and yet at the same time a dream that would move a modern audience. It is not difficult to imagine the energies the poem would have released in him, the author of Orghast, Crow and other works of channelled, intense gendered energy. His projected scenario remains faithful in its outlines to the original.

Jenny Lewis's version, which has been broadcast and performed because it is the most voice-friendly version since Edwin Morgan's theatre adaptation, responds in its formal variety, diction and changing points of view to the objection that the poem is excessively macho. It also presents Gilgamesh on a manageable scale, so that one voice can render all the parts. It allows the drama to be generated by the language, without the intrusion of stagecraft.

. . .

Scholars rightly affirm their hold on the poem, its linguistic and cultural integrity, which are at risk from the creative free-for-all that surrounds *Gilgamesh*. Benjamin Foster, whose full title is Professor of Assyrian and Babylonian Literature at Yale University, declares, 'I have no patience with clueless folk who think that they can translate the epic without going to the trouble of mastering Babylonian, though of course they are welcome to retell it.' It is a proper distinction, between retelling, and pretending to translate. As Heidegger has it, the poet makes, but does not master the medium: the poet attends to and attends for the call of language, is drawn out by it.* (The reader, also.)

A poem's original language and form are what the sense is made from. If we do not know the *language*, how can we approach the poem? When we cannot hear it except in transliteration, and even then cannot clearly infer the accentual patterning, how do we read along with it, as the critic Hélène Cixous says we must, so that the poem is alive, in dialogue with us as sound and sense? And isn't any translation, even by a scholar, and any retelling, inevitably going to be an act of limitation, constraint? Coming as it does *after* the creative event, what can it do but describe and reduce it?

Yes, but. *Gilgamesh* is a poem different in kind from any other major narrative we are likely to encounter. It does not have a creative event, an occasion, in the way that, for example, Virgil's *Aeneid* does, because it does not have an author serving an emperor in the way that the *Aeneid* did, nor in the centuries of its composition did it have a single flatterer or a single patron to flatter. It is an accretion. The Standard Babylonian, from which

* Martin Heidegger, 'The Nature of Language', in *On the Way to Language*, translated by Peter D. Hertz (New York: Harper and Row, 1971).

we take our bearings, incorporates material adapted from more ancient Old Babylonian. We supplement our understanding and fill in some of the blanks from fragments surviving in still other languages.

The poem we work with is, then, in its origins itself an enhanced translation and, after that, a scribal and then a scholarly construction. It is the product of a series of texts in which many kinds of reader, and many kinds of writer or reciter, participated over millennia. A definitive text will never be established. The poem will never stabilise. It abounds in contested readings; and, to complicate matters further, additional material that re-adjusts the poem keeps surfacing in archaeological digs, museum collections, and even on the black market in antiquities.

No wonder so many poets who are not proven translators feel free to scale the text and plant their flags at its summits. The generosity and abundance of scholarship empower readers without rudimentary Old Babylonian or Standard Babylonian to do more than just read existing versions. Benjamin Foster might agree with the novelist, scholar and critic Gabriel Josipovici, who in a letter writes that imitation, as against informed translation, is a license for laziness:

> Instead of trying to come to grips with the original somehow or other, the poet as imitator feels that the original has merely to act as a trigger for his or her own instincts. As a result, as in so much modern art, we get the sense of an unfettered subjectivity, whereas, to me, the joy of great art lies always in the sense that it is fettered, that it is struggling with the difficult business of catching the world.

Yet Foster, George and other Assyriologists, in the detail of their scholarship, release the mischievous djinn of imitation or 'translation at one remove' from the fractured lamp that is the poem. Their footnotes fill would-be translators, and critics like myself, with an illusion (is it pure illusion?) that we can get close to the original and even (mouthing the transliteration) have a distant familiarity with the sound of its language.

Interlopers achieve mixed results among the dead languages of the world. Most contemporary readers interlope. The poem is fascinating even at several removes of time and language. We hold the scholarly versions to our ears almost as though they are the originals, and we set to work. We want to *hear.*

With Benjamin Foster's strictly qualified permission, with Gabriel Josipovici's severe caveats in mind, we can pick a way through as much of the story as we have. We can re-tell it.

TABLET 1

He who saw everything, of him learn, o my land, learn

of him who sought out to know what lands are for, &
    people, to turn

to fruitfulness after the wastings and the idlenesses, the
    ways

to use what is called strength after its misuse, he who had
    tidings

of times when deltas were of use as deltas and not
    floodings of excrement . . .

Charles Olson, 'Bigmans II'

THOUGH the *Gilgamesh* texts we read are transcribed from clay tablets, the poem itself in lines 9 and 10 tells us that Gilgamesh 'came a far road, was weary, found peace, / and set all his labours on a tablet of stone' (George in 1999), or 'from a distant journey came home, weary, at peace, / Engraved all his hardships on a monument of stone' (Foster in 2001). The poem purports, then, to be the king's own story, set down by his own hand for all to read in his later, wiser years, when he had come to see the Deep, the country's foundations. Two very different scholarly editions agree on one point: Gilgamesh was at peace when, older and wiser, the tale is recounted. They also agree that, though the account is said to be his own, he does not use the first person singular or the royal 'we'.

But scholars disagree on many particulars, as though the language is blurred and each sees different figures emerging from it. George sees a 'far road' and Foster abstracts a 'distant journey'; George's active 'found' is Foster's passive 'was at'; George's light 'set down' becomes Foster's ponderous 'engraved'; and are the incidents we will read 'labours' (neutral) or 'hardships' (morally charged)? Is the 'tablet' in question something we might hold in our hands, or is it a monument?

George has made a habit of coming back to the poem again and again, debating with it and with his understanding of it, and adjusting his translation accordingly. His sense of the poem does not stand still. We have different versions of it as he reads, and—better informed, wiser—re-reads. Thus in 2012, reviewing his Penguin translation of 1999 and his monumental edition of 2003, he comes to a conclusion, based on his developing sense of the parallelisms and symmetries of the Standard Babylonian text, that is closer to Foster's. We must assume he has taken Foster on board, with his characteristic even-handedness. It is a complex semantic argument and reveals how challenging translation remains, even after a century and a half of scholarship.

The hinge of this transition, from Gilgamesh's frantic adventure to the solid immobility of the wall, is a succession of four clauses relating his homecoming (ll. 9–10). Placed deliberately at the midpoint of five four-line stanzas, these clauses contain the following four verbs: *illikamma* 'he came', *anih* 'he was exhausted', *šupšuh* 'he was put at ease', and *šakin* 'it was set'. Formerly I understood the last of these, the stative *šakin*, to be active in meaning, 'he set'.

But now I see that the usual force of the stative conjugation is more probable, and that *šakin* joins the two other statives, *anih* and *šupšuh*, in the intransitive-passive, as an emphatic announcement of inaction. Gilgamesh returns home, collapses exhausted, and can do no more. It is not he who places his story on the tablet of lapis lazuli. That is done for him, intransitive-passive *šakin*. After so long in motion, now he has arrived at a condition of stasis. The uneven distribution of the four clauses across the two lines of poetry—three crammed into 1.9, one alone in l. 10—serves to emphasize further the transition from journey to homecoming, from restless activity to calm inaction. The journey has come to a halt.

The change in terms of tone and movement is fundamental and ties the opening in more closely with the end of Tablet 11. George's re-reading brings the poem into clearer focus, but adds to our sense that a definitive reading is a long way off.

The young king Gilgamesh in both George and Foster is presented not as having repaired but actually built the walls of his city and the temple dedicated to Ishtar and Anu. But our translators evoke the walls in different terms. 'See its walls like a strand of *wool*, / view its parapet that none could copy!' says George. Foster instructs us to 'See its upper wall, whose facing gleams like copper, / Gaze at the lower course, which nothing can equal.' George is again more particular, Foster more elevated in register, and more regular in metre. For a moment we seem to be inhabiting different poems: a strand of wool, or gleaming copper? George's simile suggests the wall's receding length and connects the fortifications with the surrounding shepherd economy. Foster's simile emphasises impregnability, the king's prowess and the city's wealth. Stephanie Dalley sees the wall 'like a copper band'.

At Cambridge, I asked the Assyriologist professor Nicholas Postgate about the 'strand of wool'. He explained that it refers to a mason's thread, the kind used to make sure construction is straight. The poem is praising the meticulous straightness of the wall of Uruk, and thus the masterly workmanship of the construction. George is right about the strand but should have stretched it a bit tighter. There is no particular justification for the sun-reflecting copper in Foster. George lyricises, Foster heroises, while the poem is clear, not to say four-square, in its intention, which is to underline the workmanship that distinguishes Uruk's construction. Dalley seems set on harmonising Foster and George: she manages to approximate the image but not quite get to the sense.

All three translators, obeying the original, send us as audience (as readers) on a tour of Uruk. We are told where to go and what to look for. The rhetorical questions posed contain their own replies ('were its bricks not fired in an oven? / Did the Seven Sages not lay its foundations?'—George). We look down (the poem briefly lapsing into prose, as again at the very end of Tablet 11) on a square mile of city, a square mile of date palm groves, a square mile of clay-pit, and half a square mile of Ishtar's temple. We are tempted to imagine a grid layout. But scale rather than geometry is being evoked. It is important to register this: shapes and proportions throughout the poem, like numbers, can be misunderstood if we read implicit metaphor (the 'square' in 'a square mile') with an English preference for the literal that can be visualised.

The prologue ends at line 28 of the George translation, line 29 of the Foster. By now we have been shown the city, not the detail but the wide-angle view. At this point the scale and the tone in which we are addressed change. Having used our eyes to see, we are instructed to take something extraordinary and precious in our hands. George says:

> [*See*] the tablet-box of cedar,
>> [*release*] its clasp of bronze!
> [*Lift*] the lid of its secret,
>> [*pick*] *up* the tablet of lapis lazuli and read out
> the travails of Gilgamesh, all that he went through.

Foster says:

> [Search out] the foundation box of copper,
> [Release] its lock of bronze,
> Raise the lid upon its hidden contents,
> Take up and read from the lapis tablet
> Of him, Gilgamesh, who underwent many hardships.

The change of sense register is like a change of key in music: the poem emphasises our individual presence in those imperatives, 'See' and 'Search out', but requires our participation in the verb 'read' and 'read out'. 'Read out' suggests performance: the words are to be made into sound by our voices. We are not only to read but to speak. The poem assumes we know how to read, and it gives us an active role in narrating the script of the events that are going to be told. The poem is off, and we are in the saddle.

Or rather, the *poems* are off. Because each translation, while taking us on roughly the same road, negotiates the steeper gradients and the numerous pot-holes in different ways. Even these opening lines reveal how much scope for variation (and error) exists. The image of the poem inscribed on precious stone, a definitive version as it were, the king's own testimony, teases us, since all we possess are transcriptions from clay tablets and shards, excavated from ruins spread over several countries, several dead languages and more than two millennia; and English versions come powered by different engines and riding on different suspensions, though they purport to be based on the same time-battered Standard Babylonian prototype.

In whichever vehicle we choose to travel, it is unsettling, this start of the poem's journey. We have been told the king is 'wise in all matters' (George) or 'wise in all things' (Foster), knowing in a complex way the ground his realm is built on. He is also said to know about the antediluvian past and has stories to tell from that period. He is a builder, and even the Builder. But when the action begins he is not what the prologue advertises. He is too young to have built the massive walls of his city; his social delinquency is a far cry from wisdom.

But we run ahead of ourselves.

If we stand a little further back from the not-quite-in-sync scholarly translations, we get a clearer sense of the story. And we have to accept that the narrative is quite different from the kinds of narrative we are accustomed to, even in the Homeric poems. The perspective of the end informs the entire poem, so that though our protagonist is young and wilful when we meet him, the wise person he will become provides authority for the story from lines 9 and 10 of the first tablet. The end exists in the beginning: this analepsis is built into the narrative.

Events and dreams are not confined to their moment; their meaning comes clear only later. Dreams often occur in sequences, the later dreams confirming and expanding the first. Even in the narrative, events connect and carry by implication their consequences. Dramatic suspense is not part of the experience of

Gilgamesh. It is as though narrative is turned around, and what engages us is how the story fulfils its expected ends, or reaches its anticipated, its advertised conclusion. Bill Griffiths, in conversation with Paul Batchelor, speaks illuminatingly of the verses' 'predictive structure', a recurrent resource in our poetic traditions:

> I looked back at transcripts of the original cuneiform, to see what was happening. It's basically a balanced line, similar to the Psalms, with a repetition of sense in the two halves of the line: sense rhythm. Many passages in the Bible are pure poetry: the Lord's Prayer, the Sermon on the Mount, the Psalms. . . . It comes back again in Christopher Smart, and Walt Whitman. It's limited, in that it's still a predictive structure, but it's interesting—it widens our palette.

· · ·

The story begins. The ancient city of Uruk-the-Sheepfold is ruled by a young king. He is two-thirds god (his mother was the divine Ninsun, 'Lady Wild Cow') and one-third man (we will return to his father Lugalbanda, 'Little Lord' or 'Shepherd', one-time king of Uruk). The young king's name is Gilgamesh. The meaning of his name is uncertain. It may in Sumerian signify 'the ancestor is a youth'. We first encounter him as young, though when we leave him at the poem's end he has become the mature player promised to us in the opening lines, 'wise in all matters'.

He is not yet a good king. In fact, in Tablet 1, he is a king behaving badly. Proud of his strength, he likes to wrestle. He makes the young men of Uruk wrestle with him day after day. He wears them out. Even when they have other things to do, he makes them fight with him. He always wins because he is the king—also, as we have seen, because he is enormous in comparison to them. He is hardly challenged by these combats.

He has a worse habit. Whenever a young man is going to get married, who turns up at the nuptials but the sexually primed young king, who makes it his business to have his way with the bride-to-be. This is, he says, his right. No one is strong enough to stop him.

The women of Uruk do not like his conduct. They go to the temple and pray to the gods to devise some way of checking the king's *kukittu*, his depraved behaviour. They do not want to kill him: they are loyal subjects, and in those days you did not depose or kill bad leaders, you worked with the gods to find ways of making them better. The women pray, and the gods, who are always close at hand in Uruk, and receive people's prayers and tributes in their temples, heed the faithful petitioners. They confer with one another and devise a way to check the overweening 'ancestor is a youth'. Action, albeit oblique action, will be taken.

Anu, the Father God, enjoins Aruru, the Mother Goddess, to act. (The passage with Anu's words has been lost from the Standard Babylonian texts so far discovered, so the scholars add it back from an older text. It happily survived in an exercise copy made by an apprentice scribe.) Aruru, having first washed her hands, 'takes a pinch of clay' and throwing it, as a potter might throw a lump onto the wheel, fashions Enkidu in the wilderness. She is helped by vigorous Ninurta, the god of agriculture, who is handsome and, existing outside time, forever young, not like Gilgamesh, who, if we take the proffered etymology of his name, was young only in his youth.

Enkidu, the fruit of Aruru's and Ninurta's efforts, is a hairy man. His whole body is furred over. He is like other animals of the wild. The hair on his head, thanks to Ninurta's contribution, grows thick as grain. At his introduction the poem seems to enter a sort of lyric present before reverting, when we return to Uruk, to the past tense.

Enkidu knows the beasts of the field. He grazes with the gazelles and goes down on all fours to drink at the water-hole. He is very large and very strong.

On three successive days a trapper—in the Hittite version of *Gilgamesh* he is named Shangashush—spots Enkidu at the water-hole. Terrified, he tells his father, guessing that it must be this creature who fills in his pit-traps and frees beasts from the trappers' snares. His father sends him to Uruk to find King Gilgamesh and tell his story. He urges him to bring back Shamhat, a hierodule or consecrated *fille de joie* (I am reluctant, given her central role in the poem, and her generous disposition, to call her a 'temple harlot'), to seduce the wild man and lure him into the human orbit. This is generally presented as 'civilising' Enkidu: the pacific vegetarian who is as close to nature as a free-roaming gazelle, a friend of the beasts of the field, is civilised when he has intercourse and goes to town, becoming a warrior.

Again, we are running ahead.

• • •

Uruk is three days distant from the water-hole, but the journey does not matter. As in the Bible, details that are not crucial to the moral plot are left out, the time of mere contingencies passing in a flash. The young trapper easily locates Gilgamesh in the city. There's no mistaking the king who towers over everyone else and is always looking for a fight. Gilgamesh listens to what Shangashush has to say and then repeats, almost verbatim, the words the trapper's father used, instructing him to conduct Shamhat the hierodule to the water-hole to seduce the large hairy human creature, socialise him, and bring him back to Uruk.

As noted earlier, the speech one person delivers is often repeated word for word by another who has clearly not been present when the speech was first uttered. It is as though certain speeches are appropriate to certain encounters, and anyone who has to deliver them will happen on the same set of words, the right template. The place of repetition in *Gilgamesh* is one of its formal peculiarities. It may have had to do with the oral-formulaic origins of the poem, repetition being a basic mnemonic. But if we are not persuaded that *Gilgamesh* is oral-formulaic in origin, there are other explanations, which tie in with the world-view of the poem, its patterned form and its larger themes, which we will come to later.

The hierodule Shamhat, unresisting (there is no discussion, no persuasion, no dramatic interplay between her and the young trapper), leaves her temple and goes with Shangashush. It takes them three days to get to the water-hole. (The poem tells us how much time has elapsed but again does not describe the journey, which—entertaining as it might have been—is unimportant to the poem.)

Shangashush positions Shamhat, knees apart, her sex exposed to view, at the brink of the water where Enkidu is sure to see her. It takes three days for Enkidu to appear. Then, sure enough, her displayed charms begin to work. In due course they see and smell one another. Thereupon Enkidu spends six days and seven nights in the focused pleasure of sexual initiation and reiteration.

What translators make of this short passage tells us whether or not they are attuned to the poem, which is at all points thrifty and precise. Later we will view Shamhat and Enkidu from the angles taken by several translations, some of them lighting the scene luridly, as though Shamhat had strayed in from a blue movie.

His energy sapped, after seven nights Enkidu can no longer keep up with the wild flock, and the animals, companions since he was first created, turn away from him. Now Shamhat flatters him. She compares him to a god and proposes to take him to Uruk to see the temples and to meet and challenge the king who, she tells him, has seen dreams, one of a comet falling at his feet and one of an enormous axe. The comet and the axe represent his impending meeting with Enkidu.

In *Gilgamesh* the actors *see* a dream, they do not dream it: the dream has an objective significance: it is intended to disclose something about the fixed future. Dreams never speak directly. They require interpreting. You take your dream to the temple, or to your mother if she is a goddess, and you ask for an explanation. A dream is never just a function of your psyche or an accident of digestion; it is never subjective, because in ancient Uruk notions of subjectivity are not yet even a rumour within the city's walls.

Shamhat tells Enkidu that Gilgamesh has asked his goddess mother to interpret the two dreams, and she has told him he can expect the arrival of a hitherto unknown intimate friend. Shamhat's access to Gilgamesh's dreams and to his conversations with his divine mother are not explained, but she is a holy person, come from the temple, and she *knows*; and she is Enkidu's first human contact, so he believes her.

Shamhat washes and tidies him up: Enkidu the wild man gets his hair, or his pelt, put in order. For the scholarly translator Stephanie Dalley, Enkidu's hair is not as woolly and virile as it appears to be in some other versions. She agrees with George, portraying him as more tressy than Esau-like and pelty. Long-messy locks prove comb-able rather than curled and snagged. Certainly Shamhat's ease in transforming his looks supports the view that he is, once bathed, much less intractably wild and virile than he at first seemed.

Dalley's reading, more deliberately than George's, paves the way for the suggestion of a Uranian relationship between Enkidu and Gilgamesh. Some contemporary gay writers and readers cheerfully buy into this reading even though the six days and seven nights of clearly heterosexual lovemaking in Tablet 1 are repeated at the start of Tablet 2, and no account is given in the poem of homosexual acts. The gay poet and critic Greg Woods makes no claims but gently affirms, 'I keep *Gilgamesh* on a (mental) shelf with other lamentations—Achilles for Patroclus, David for Jonathan, Roland for Olivier—and the tradition of pastoral elegy from Bion's "Lament for Adonis", through Milton's "Lycidas", to *The Waste Land* and on.' That measured response allows for the possibility without insisting on it.

A conventional take on the poem is possible, though it is not fanciful to see Enkidu as a pliant creation. He is shaped out of clay in response to the women of Uruk's prayer, to deflect Gilgamesh's unwanted and aggressively heterosexual attentions. Why should Gilgamesh not be drawn in another direction when the opportunity arises, especially if he is no longer permitted to ravage brides-to-be? Also, Enkidu is portrayed as someone constructed to Gilgamesh's own scale. But such reflections are too literal for the poem, which says as much as it means. We have no cause to doubt Shamhat's or Enkidu's heterosexual proficiency and stamina. The declared acts of intimacy between Enkidu and Gilgamesh are confined in the poem to hand-holding and kisses, whatever the voices off might be whispering. Modern readers cock their ears to the voices off and hear what they want to hear, which is not to say that their hearing is wrong, only that it cannot be proven right from the poem as we currently have it—unless we turn to the twelfth tablet, which most scholars agree does not belong with the first eleven, though it is hard to ignore it altogether.

After Shamhat has described Gilgamesh's dreams to Enkidu, one of two things is said. Shamhat tells Enkidu that he and Gilgamesh will be drawn together by love, or the poem tells us that Shamhat and Enkidu will resume their sexual activity. The Standard Babylonian text seems to offer a choice. It's possible that both things are conveyed at once and it is unnecessary for readers to plump for a single meaning: Enkidu and Shamhat make love, and she promises him the comradeship of Gilgamesh to come.

Dalley says, 'Thus Shamhat heard the dreams of Gilgamesh and told them to Enkidu. / "[The dreams mean that you will lo]ve one another."' George is equally categorical in taking the poem in another direction: '[After] Shamhat had told Enkidu the dreams of Gilgamesh, / the two of them together [began making] love.' The square brackets for each translator work to different ends.

What matters is that Gilgamesh's divine mother, interpreting the first dream, in which the not yet present Enkidu appears as a fallen comet, describes him as 'one who can save the life of a friend', and the second dream, of the copper axe (prefiguring, perhaps, the visit to the cedar forest and the chopping down of the great trees), as 'one who can save the life of a comrade'. Even as Gilgamesh is reporting the axe dream to his mother, Enkidu squats entranced before Shamhat the hierodule, a synchronicity which adds to the 'predictive' patterning and to our sense that what happens is determined, not willed.

The first tablet introduces a wide range of players and a wealth of incidents. The story is briskly told in a condensed three hundred lines. The trapper goes to Uruk in the twinkling of an eye: 'He took the road, set [his face] towards Uruk,' George's version reads, and then instantly, '*before* Gilgamesh *the king [he spoke these words]*.' Gilgamesh instructs him, and again without further ado,

> Off went the hunter, taking Shamhat the harlot,
>> they set out on the road, they started the journey.
> On the third day they came to their destination,
>> hunter and harlot sat down there *to wait.*

The narrative could not be more austere.

I generally speak of 'players' or 'figures' rather than 'characters' in *Gilgamesh*. Character suggests psychological and emotional dimensions strictly anachronistic (*pace* Ted Hughes) in the context of *Gilgamesh*, even in relation to Enkidu and Gilgamesh himself. 'Players' emphasises the dramatic relations between figures who lack significant interiority, and the abundance of repetitive, stylised dialogue. At times we might imagine that we are reading an ancient play script and not an ancient poem. 'Players' delays our trying to identify motive and to attribute feelings that have little bearing on the original. Both players overcome their weaknesses without too much of a struggle, through dialogue and repetition. They express rather stiffly what the story requires them to feel.

Enkidu is subject to human change and growth, and he comes closest of the figures in the poem to having a definable character. Gilgamesh, for his part, becomes less churlish and more human through the narrative. In the end he fulfils the opening promise of the poem: he sees the deep and grows wise in all matters.

If Gilgamesh is, even remotely, based on a historical king, Enkidu seems to be a child of pure fiction. His and Gilgamesh's relationship, whatever its intended nature, is emblematic of the ways in which narrative fact requires the complementarity of invention and its illuminating irony, to find the sense in it. Fiction throws a raking light over fact; it also projects the shadows that make for three-dimensionality in an otherwise flattened chronicle. Enkidu puts us in mind of Hamlet's Horatio in the ways he draws out and completes the hero.

The scale of Gilgamesh's kingdom is defined in the first and second tablets. We look down on the city of Uruk from the walls. We see the city's proportions. For the trapper travelling to ask Gilgamesh for advice, the distance from the countryside to the city is three days (distance being measured by the time it takes to traverse, not by the miles travelled). He makes his way without distraction, straight into the young king's presence.

At the risk of marring narrative continuity, we note that the second tablet, in which Enkidu learns his second (eating bread) and third (drinking beer) lessons in being human, portrays the shepherds. Though they do not live in Uruk, they know Gilgamesh: they compare Enkidu's build familiarly with the king's, and they affirm the two men's equal physical prowess. This enhances the sense of a close-knit kingdom, the humble folk knowing and known to the king, the countryside and the city communicating freely one with the other, and each dependent on the other.

And the people are close to their gods, too: the gods are as near as neighbours. In fact, they are neighbours, nosy and helpful and sometimes vindictive like neighbours. The distances between those who do not die (the gods) and those who do (their subjects) could be measured with a good pedometer. What sets the gods apart is time: Gilgamesh who 'has been a youth', for example, is a youth no longer (his name confirming he is mortal); the god Ninurta is always young and, though he enters and affects events *in* time, has his existence outside it, with Aruru and fellow gods. Ishtar, we shall discover, can enjoy a succession of mortal lovers, playthings she can punish, discard or kill. She does not grow old but remains insatiably perched on time's shore, plucking out of the stream the lovers she will use, maim and then throw back.

TABLET 2

[Enkidu] was a man.

And when beer and cooked meats

Were placed before him

He stared at them as the animals had stared at him

Dressed in his new language.

Alan Wall, *Gilgamesh*

ENKIDU gets carried away in his sexual transports with Shamhat. She tells him he is godlike and persuades him to go to Uruk. She divides her ample clothing between the two of them.

(The opening lines of the second tablet are damaged, but a text that survives in Old Babylonian seems to fit, and George interpolates it here.) Shamhat leads Enkidu, now tidied up, smoothed, combed and dressed, to the shepherds' encampment. The shepherds marvel at his dimensions, his strength, his good looks. He is built like the king himself, solid as a fortress.

For the first time in his life he is presented with human food and drink. He tastes bread and learns to eat it. (There is another fault in the tablet, filled in by scholars resorting to the Old Babylonian sources once more. Indeed, the Old Babylonian and the Standard Babylonian texts work together, as if in conversation, for the remainder of this tablet.)

The shepherds give him beer. He quaffs seven goblets.

Among the shepherds he makes it his job at night to protect the flocks from the wild beasts, his erstwhile companions.

He could readily have made his home among the shepherds, but a passer-by, interrupting another night of lovemaking with Shamhat, tells how in Uruk King Gilgamesh is continuing to claim first-night rights with the young brides. Enkidu is enraged (having rapidly developed a sense of moral propriety since he has become sexual). He sets out to put an end to this practice, taking Shamhat with him. Now he, not she, takes the lead.

The people of Uruk are amazed at his stature and strength, how like Gilgamesh he is, though a little shorter and a little broader of build. (We are not told how many cubits separate *his* nipples.) He is the answer to the women's prayers, and they choose him as a champion. They pay him deep homage. He has been decisively socialised.

At their first encounter Enkidu blocks Gilgamesh on his way to a bridal assignation. They launch into a tremendous fight, violent and protracted, a kind of earthquake. Neither prevails, but Enkidu speaks to Gilgamesh and the king listens. What he says is lost in the breakages of time, but whatever words he uses persuade Gilgamesh to stop ravaging brides-to-be and cements their comradeship. At the conclusion of their fight, 'They kissed each other and made friends,' says Foster's translation. Another gap follows in which Gilgamesh presents Enkidu to his mother Ninsun, the Wild Cow. From the few words we can still hear on the tablets, she is not pleased. She finds her son's friend shaggy, unkempt; he has no father, no relations. Enkidu is reduced to tears.

It is into these and other vulnerable gaps in the text that the inventive interpolator can read a variety of possibilities, some more credible than others. Edwin Morgan in his dramatic adaptation at this point queers the heroes, in a spirit of cheerful anachronism.

When the story confidently resumes, Gilgamesh, to restore his new friend's spirits after Ninsun's disapproval, comes up with his plan for an adventure. They will go to the cedar forest, home of the guardian monster Humbaba. They will defeat him and fell the trees, bringing them back to use for construction in Uruk. Enkidu at first opposes the plan. He knows the forest: sixty leagues of wilderness. He knows fiery Humbaba from his wild days. 'Humbaba, his voice is the Deluge,' says Enkidu twice, a line taken up later by the elders. He and they associate Humbaba with Adad the storm god. This may prefigure Uta-napishti's account of the great flood in the eleventh tablet. In short, Enkidu, the chorus of elders and young men affirm that the guardian of the cedar forest is not to be meddled with. The journey is long, mapless, unpredictable.

Gilgamesh pooh-poohs such cowardice. His aim in life is to gain lasting fame, to prove himself. His vaunting hubris no one can curb. So the king and his new friend have weapons forged, and huge hatchets to fell the woods. The copy of the second tablet held in the Yale University Library is quite specific about the weight and value of the hatchets. Since the written languages of Sumer and Akkad were originally devised to record quantities and values and itemise commercial transactions, habits of valuation persist in the chronicles and spill over into the poetry.

The king convenes a meeting in the centre of Uruk. He laughs at the elders and youths when they urge caution. He will have his way. When he returns, he vows, there will be two celebrations of the New Year (The end of the tablet has vanished, interrupting Gilgamesh in an over-reaching speech.)

Stephanie Dalley suggests that in the Old Babylonian account of the forest adventure, the heroes set out not for Lebanon, to the west, but for the eastern mountains where not cedar but pine was their quarry. Certainly between the Sumerian and the Akkadian periods there was a geographical re-orientation, but even in Old Babylonian times trade went west to the Mediterranean. It seems likely that the narrative eyes of the poem turned west from the outset. There is no doubt that the Standard Babylonian poem faces west.

TABLET 3

Rimat-Ninsun, the mother of Gilgamesh,

in the company of the votaries of the temple,
spoke and said to Enkidu the companion,

placing a sacred pendant about his neck:
'Though not my son, here I adopt you son,

not to forsake my son in the future danger.'
Then from the Seven-Bolt Gate the two departed,

hearing the warnings and blessings of the city.

David Ferry, *Gilgamesh: A New Rendering in English Verse*

SINCE Gilgamesh is determined, the elders resign themselves to his departure. They urge him to depend on his comrade Enkidu, who knows the way and should go in front, protecting his friend. In Foster they enjoin Enkidu: 'Let him return, to be a grave husband,' and Dalley says, 'Let Enkidu . . . bring him back safe in person for brides,' suggesting in a footnote a subtlety Foster has incorporated without comment: 'Pun perhaps: "brides/graves", *hirtu, hiratu* "bride", *hiritu* "grave", both with plural *hirati*.' George has simply, 'Enkidu shall bring him safe home to his *wives*!' Each paints rather a different picture: Foster suggests he will come home to wed; Dalley that he will return to marry several wives and/or die several deaths; George that he may already be married to several women. We know what a scourge he was to other men's brides-to-be before Enkidu arrived. Neither warrior is provided with even one spouse in what survives of the poem, though Gilgamesh fatefully rejects one proposal of marriage.

The king and his companion go hand in hand to Ninsun's temple, to secure the goddess's blessing. After she has gone through a thorough ritual cleansing, no fewer than seven baths at the bath house, still reluctantly, but fully decked in her finery, she goes up onto the flat roof of her temple dwelling and conducts a ceremony, enjoining Shamash, god of the Sun, in his circuit, daily to support her son in his quest; and Aya the dawn, the Sun's wife, to assist. Ninsun seems to anticipate her son's deification—'Will he not share the heavens with you?' she asks Shamash, 'Will he not share with the moon a sceptre and crown?' Shamash does not answer, but we know this will not be, as far as the poem is concerned. Gilgamesh's wish for a god's life outside time is not granted. Shamash touches on the theme of what will come, upon Enkidu's death, to her son's quest. Her other prayers are more favourably answered.

Now she adopts Enkidu, and marks him as her foster child.

(The tablet is very damaged and there are no useful alternative versions to go by.)

Gilgamesh and Enkidu make sacrifices. Gilgamesh leaves instructions for the governing of Uruk in his absence. The city officials then advise the king on how he should go, echoing the words of the elders. Enkidu, persuaded, urges Gilgamesh forward, and to the cheers of the young men—Enkidu tells Gilgamesh to turn them back, since they are clearly minded to follow the heroes on their adventure—they set out alone for the cedar forest. Or so we assume: the tablet is broken off.

As they leave the city, as we with them leave the kingdom of Uruk with its high walls, its surrounding pastures and wilds, physical space itself seems to expand. We move off the map into the unknown. The poem will take us further out with each adventure.

TABLET 4

'He who leads the way preserves himself

And keeps his companion safe.

Though they may perish,

Yet their name will endure.'

And so they both arrived at the green mountain.

They fell silent and stood quite still.

Robert Temple, *He Who Saw Everything*

THE trip to the Cedar Mountain is long, even for such powerful, young, fleet-footed comrades. Depending on the translation, they travel twenty leagues (sixty miles) or double leagues (120 miles) and have lunch, then another thirty (ninety miles) or sixty (180 miles) before pitching camp. In three days they cover a distance that most would have taken a month and a half to cross.

Their entire journey lasts (probably) six nights and seven days. They have to cross seven mountains or mountain ranges. Each night, when they pitch camp, they dig a hole, pour water in as an offering to the parched underworld—one of the promises they made on their departure—and Gilgamesh climbs to a high point to make an offering of flour which he pours out, praying to the mountain to give him a dream omen. In each camp Enkidu builds the king a snug house to dream in, positions him within a circle (of flour?) that he has drawn, 'and *falling flat* like a net lays himself in the doorway'.

Gilgamesh, who we already know is prone to see symbolic dreams, sleeps with his chin on his knees. He experiences what seems to him a series of alarming nightmares. In the first a mountain falls upon him. In the second (if we accept the earlier Middle Babylonian telling, from a tablet found in Hattusa) the mountain grabs him by the feet and a handsome, luminous man appears who pulls him free and sets him on his way. In the third, lightning, darkness, flames, a fire of death (as if a volcano had erupted) terrify him. The fourth dream (if we credit an Old Babylonian tablet from Nippur) involves a Thunderbird rising up and breathing fire, a Thunderbird (Humbaba foreshadowed) which is restrained and bound by a man. The fifth dream (we turn to another Old Babylonian tablet from ancient Shaduppûm) is of an enormous bull that Gilgamesh has taken by the horns. A further dream is lost. In each case Enkidu gives the dream a positive spin and turns it in an encouraging direction. The man who comes and saves Gilgamesh he identifies as Shamash, the Sun himself, who has given them permission and promised them protection.

He is offered water to drink by his father Lugalbanda, now a god.

(We return to Tablet 4.)

The cedar forest is near at hand and Gilgamesh is feeling, frankly, uneasy. But because the gods are always close by their protégés, Shamash calls aloud to him from the sky. He urges Gilgamesh and Enkidu to strike immediately, before Humbaba has time to enter the forest where the seven (in the Hittite, eight) auras, splendours, cloaks, mantles, terrors or glories (depending on the translation), in which he can wrap himself and which he can send out to defend himself, will make him impregnable and prove fatal to them. Or are they seven sons? In one Old Babylonian version these—whatevers—are not slain but run wild into the woods after Humbaba is taken.

As they approach, Humbaba is audible, trumpeting from his territory.

The men gather courage. Having come such a long way over the difficult mountains, this is no time to be faint-hearted. They still their trembling knees, and movement returns to their fear-stiffened limbs. They join hands and fare forward towards Humbaba's forest. As the tablet ends, they come to a halt at the edge of the forest.

TABLET 5

He stood still watching as the monster leaned to make

His final strike against his friend, unable

To move to help him, and then Enkidu slid

Around the ground like a ram making its final lunge

On wounded knees. Humbaba fell and seemed

To crack the ground itself in two, and Gilgamesh

As if this fall had snapped him from his daze

Returned to life . . .

Herbert Mason, *Gilgamesh: A Verse Narrative*

TABLET 5 appears from archaeological remains to have been among the least frequently copied of all the tablets, which is surprising given its exotic content. It is more dramatic and arresting than some of the preceding tablets, and a young scribe might have felt as though his tedious copying duties were lightened by the detail of the story, the excitement of a landscape full of strange creatures and so wonderfully lush in an often-parched world. There were, however, few instances of such relief for the labouring apprentice.

The forest is high, deep and dense, with a mountain in the centre, a throne for the gods. Humbaba has made paths through it. Gilgamesh and Enkidu admire the trees and the creatures that inhabit them. In a portion of the poem preserved in the Sulaymaniyah Museum, Iraq, and translated in 2007 by F.N.H. Al-Rawi and Andrew George, and by Benjamin Foster in 2017, this is what we are shown:

> The cedar was dappled sixty cubits high with
> incrustation,
> The resin [oozed] out, dribbling down like raindrops,
> It [flowed into a torrent] and ditches carried it away.
> Throughout the forest birdlife was chirping,
> . . . answering each other in rhythmic din . . .
> A pigeon was cooing, a turtledove answering,
> The forest was joyous with the [cry] of the stork,
> The forest was abundantly joyous from the [lilt] of the
> francolin.
> Mother monkeys kept up their calls, baby monkeys
> squeaked . . .
> Like a band of musicians and drummers,
> They resounded all day long in the presence of
> Humbaba . . .

Descriptions of this kind are uncommon in the brisk, thrifty movement of Standard Babylonian poetry. They bring the story to a stand, and, with the protagonists, we wonder at the place they are entering. Exaggerated in its lushness and in its material value (the resin oozing from the trees in such abundance is precious amber, and amber was sourced from Lebanon), it adds to the visual a kind of allegorical charge. Here are the cedar trees that will be felled, this is the unspoiled environment that will be destroyed when its guardian Humbaba is killed. The word

'joyous' is repeated; there is a pattern to the music of the crea-
tures. It is hard not to see Humbaba as benign, with these natu-
ral phenomena flourishing in his presence, under his aegis. The
impact of this passage, setting the scene for the carnage to
follow, is complex and otherworldly.

The comrades advance cautiously, weapons in hand. And here
at last is Humbaba himself, defender of his luxuriant, perfumed
and peaceful kingdom, a more eloquent monster than we antici-
pated. He does not only make terrifying noises; he speaks, and
he speaks the very language that Gilgamesh and Enkidu speak
also. He scorns Enkidu, who had no parents ('you spawn of a fish,
who knew no father, / hatchling of terrapin and turtle, who
sucked no mother's milk!'), and damns him for betraying him to
Gilgamesh. He threatens the young king, promising to feed his
body parts to the carrion birds.

Gilgamesh is first afraid (as is Enkidu). 'We have come to a
place where a man shouldn't go . . .'. The perils are suddenly real.
Despite Humbaba's rage, Gilgamesh feels something—is it an in-
stinct of compassion? or mercy? or is it guilt that what they are
about to do is wrong?—and pauses. Humbaba is after all the ser-
vant of Enlil, 'Lord Wind', the divine ruler of earth and of hu-
mankind, a higher deity than Shamash, the Sun, patron of the
comrades' expedition.

Shamash knows where they are and what they need. He des-
patches thirteen powerful winds to hinder Humbaba, who is keen
to escape with his auras into the dense forest and do battle there,
where he will stand every chance of victory, or at least survival.
The winds ranged against him blow from the four cardinal points,
winds of every intensity, bursting in his face to blind him. (In
the Old Babylonian, Shamash sends seven winds, in the Hittite
eight, drawing on different numerological traditions.) Sure

enough, Humbaba is trapped. He cannot go forward or back, and Gilgamesh, with his weapons drawn, begins his attack.

Enkidu urges him on, his speech preserved partly on an Old Babylonian tablet. They must act quickly before Enlil hears what they are up to. They know they are transgressing into a space that is properly his, but they must complete what they have begun or themselves fall before Humbaba. After his moment's backsliding, Enkidu becomes the voice of courage itself.

The king attacks, the monster struggles back. Vulnerable now, Humbaba flatters Gilgamesh and begs to be spared. He tries to bribe him with promises of a supply of lumber. Again Gilgamesh wavers, again Enkidu urges him to slay Humbaba immediately, before Enlil hears the din and acts. Humbaba then tries to flatter Enkidu, he wheedles, he promises submission, but to no avail.

They move in for the kill.

Humbaba loudly curses them, and then, stabbed in the neck by Gilgamesh, he is felled with three blows. Enkidu pulls out his lungs. (Then details are added from an Old Babylonian tablet from Ishchali.) The auras disperse. ('My friend, catch a bird and where go its chicks?') The (seven) auras will be dealt with later. There is an earthquake; the streambeds flow with gore.

The two friends start to harvest the cedars. Seven giant trees are felled and bound in the forest. Enkidu promises to construct a great door in Uruk from one of the grandest trees, for the entrance to the Temple of Enlil, the god whose servant they have slain and whose forest they have violated, and who, with Anu and Aruru and Ea the god of the water table, supremely governs the world. Enlil's gates we might imagine as being in scale something like the great reconstructed Balawat Gates in the British Museum, recovered at Imgur-Enlil and shipped back to England by Hormuzd Rassam in 1878, along with cuneiform tablets and other ancient artefacts. Maureen Kovacs translates the gate vow on these terms:

> 'My friend, we have cut down the towering Cedar whose
>   top scrapes the sky.
> Make from it a door 72 cubits high, 24 cubits wide,
> one cubit thick, its fixture, its lower and upper pivots will
>   be out of one piece.
> Let them carry it to Nippur, the Euphrates will carry it
>   down, Nippur will rejoice . . .'

The comrades make a raft of cedar logs to bear their lumber booty. Enkidu takes the helm. Gilgamesh carries as his trophy the severed head of Humbaba.

It would be interesting to know which waterway connected the remains of the cedar forest with Uruk, itself situated on a channel off the Euphrates. They had a long, hard journey to get to the cedar forest. How did they get home so swiftly? Is Stephanie Dalley right, and was Humbaba's forest of pine, not cedar, to the east, in which case more convenient waterways might be at hand? But before we allow ourselves to be literal-minded, we must remember that this is not a poem of answerable maps. Things happen, and we attend. We should not look too deeply into the geography, the logic, or the plot continuities of the narrative. Such questions are not relevant to the poem before us. Its own geography, built up over more than a millennium, spurns the demands of the contemporary travel-reader. The challenge for us as readers and interpreters, Ford Madox Ford suggested in *Return to Yesterday* (1931), is to 'keep oneself out of it'. It's hard to do, but if we succeed, we 'may present a picture of a sort of world and time'.

In a suggestive research paper, 'The Journey towards Death: The Cedar Forest in *Gilgameš* and Descriptions of the

Netherworld', the Assyriologist Selena Wisnom relates the open-
ing of Tablet 5 to other Standard Babylonian texts. She says,

> To read intertextually is to read in context—to be aware of
> the networks of meaning that certain elements of the text
> are embedded in and to interpret their meaning accord-
> ingly. No text is an island, so to speak, for it derives its
> meaning from its relation to other texts.

She brings into focus a number of issues regarding readership
(implied in the word 'text' and in the term 'intertextuality') ver-
sus audience. If *Gilgamesh* was intended for oral performance,
how conscious would the performer be of the words' relations
to specific passages in other poems, and would this conscious-
ness be communicated in performance to an audience, itself in
some way informed? Are these elements of connection, this weave
of the poem from the strands of other, earlier poems, part of
the poem's meaning, necessary for interpretation, and part of a
composer's intention? Are we reading from modernist perspec-
tives and making modernist assumptions about the nature of
authorship, textual connection and allusion in *Gilgamesh*?

This is not to suggest that the elements, or echoes, are not in
the poem; but are they there as part of a non-communicating cre-
ative design (like the concealed steel frame underlying a stone-
clad building), or do they say something about the quality not
only of composition but of at least some of the culture of recep-
tion, the elite, or the religious, or the courtly, or whatever indi-
vidual or community *Gilgamesh* addresses?

Wisnom remains focused on the kinds of intertextual relation
that might be detected, from glancing allusion to more sustained
connections. The question might be complemented from the
other side, that of readers or auditors who remain ghostly at the

edge of her argument. If we could identify them, we would go a long way towards confirming Wisnom's suggestive intuitions. But we have only ourselves to consult, and we cannot answer categorically until we locate an author in the poem, or evidence of what an ancient readership or audience attending to it might have looked like.

TABLET 6

šá ku-uṣ-ṣi el-pe-tu ku-tùm-mu-ú-⌜a⌝

at-ti taš-mi-ma an-na-a qa-ba-a-šu

tam-ḫa-ṣi-šu a-na dal-la-li tu-ut-ter-ri-šu

tu-še-ši-bi-šu-ma ina qa-bal ma-na-[ ]

ul e-lu-ú mi-iḫ-ḫul a-rid da-l[u(-)x x x x]

Transliteration from Tablet 6

GILGAMESH and Enkidu do not receive a heroes' welcome when they return to Uruk. The crowd that saw them off is absent. The sense that the poem conveyed of a busy, peopled city gives way to a different scene, almost as though they had returned to quite another poem. It is not a ghost town, but the inhabitants seem to have lost agency. When they appear, they gape.

At the beginning of Tablet 6, Gilgamesh is washing his very long and dirty hair and his headband. (The washing and tending to hair is a recurrent motif in the poem, from the moment Shamhat combs and tidies up Enkidu in preparation for socialising him.) Gilgamesh shakes his locks loose down his back, and tosses his dirty garments aside and puts on clean ones, then a cloak and a sash. He sets his crown on his head.

The goddess Ishtar watches him. She is beside herself with yearning. She cuts to the chase and immediately proposes marriage to him: 'Grant me your fruits, O grant me!' she exclaims in

fulsome Victorian strains, in George's translation. She is less fig-
urative in Foster: 'Come, Gilgamesh, you shall be my bride-
groom! / Give, oh give me your lusciousness!' Dalley is forth-
right and idiomatic: 'Come to me, Gilgamesh, and be my lover!
/ Bestow on me the gift of your fruit.' In exchange for the gift of
his fruit she will give him a spectacularly heavy chariot (made
of gold, lapis lazuli and amber) drawn by enormous mules and
lions. He will receive tribute from all the corners of the earth,
his livestock will yield triplets and twins, his horses will be extra
fast and his oxen extra strong.

Her inducement recalls Humbaba's offer of a bribe to Gil-
gamesh, if only he would spare him. She is equally unsuccessful.
Gilgamesh knows better than to be tempted. He declines this
offer from the goddess and proceeds to remind her that (in Fos-
ter's words) '[You are a brazier that goes out] when it freezes, /
A flimsy door that keeps out neither wind nor draught, / A pal-
ace that crushes a warrior . . .' He recalls her earlier marriages
and lovers. Remember, he says, Dumuzi; and the speckled *allallu-*
bird whose wing you broke, so that it cries aloud *my wing my
wing*; and the lion, for whom you set many snares; and the horse
you condemned to spur and lash; and the shepherd you turned
into a wolf, who is now harried by his own hounds; and Ishul-
lanu the gardener, turned into a dwarf.

Irish poet Thomas McCarthy told me that this passage stayed
with him most powerfully from his first reading of the poem:

> The gardener who was transformed into a frog, the shep-
> herd who was turned into a bird with a broken wing, and
> the goat-herd who was transformed into a wolf—all ruined
> just because they responded to a goddess's devouring needs:
> that seemed unfair to me at the time and fitted in perfectly
> with my experience of lovers up to that moment.

For over fifty angry lines, one of the longest sustained speeches in the poem, Gilgamesh berates Ishtar. Is his rancour proportionate? It certainly alludes to a host of legends, each one implicating her in a long history of lusts, abuses and infidelities. He does not spare her at all. This tactlessness compounds the other offences he and Enkidu by their deeds have given to the gods.

In Ishtar's view, Gilgamesh certainly protests too much. She makes no direct reply to him. She rises straight to the summit of heaven and complains shrilly to her father, Anu, and her mother, Antu. She uses a petulant little girl's language, colloquial and would-be endearing. Anu (who is the father of all the gods) reminds her that she gave the provocation in the first place. Even so, she demands from him the Bull of Heaven so she can kill Gilgamesh in his own house. But, says Anu, if the Bull of Heaven is handed over to her, there will be seven years of famine. Ishtar says she has made provision, having warehoused enough grain to see Uruk through such a crisis.

In response to her demands, he eventually agrees to lend her the fire-breathing bull (who will become the constellation *Taurus*), as a weapon with which to kill the man who has offended her. He puts in Ishtar's hands the bull's nose-rope and she leads him away.

The bull does his worst in Uruk, searing the trees, reed beds and marshes with his breath, and drinking the river till it is almost dry (the conditions of extreme drought). He makes pits with his snorts (three pits, one after the other—earthquakes?) and the men of Uruk (who reappear for this scene) fall into them, a hundred in the first pit, two hundred in the second; Enkidu himself falls waist deep into the third. He leaps out and takes the bull by the horns, tests its strength, then takes it by the tail, and Gilgamesh slaughters it. This is the second would-be deathless creature, servant of a god, which they have slain.

The bull's heart they present to Shamash, the Sun god who attended the comrades on their journey to the cedar forest. They prostrate themselves before him, then sit down side by side as equal comrades.

When, from the high walls of Uruk, Ishtar starts shouting and railing that Gilgamesh has killed the Bull of Heaven, Enkidu tears off a haunch or, some suggest, a more intimate part of the dead bull, and hurls it at Ishtar. He curses her, saying that if he could catch her he would mete out the same fate to her.

Ishtar formally mourns over the Bull of Heaven's haunch, assisted by the hierodules, prostitutes and harlots of the city. Gilgamesh takes the bull's enormous horns, has the local craftsmen decorate them with lapis lazuli, and presents them at the temple of Lugalbanda, his father, as containers to hold anointing oil. He hangs them in Lugalbanda's sleeping room.

Lugalbanda is described as a god. If he has been deified, then Gilgamesh, whose mother is a goddess, might arguably be seen as 100 percent divine, though if his father was deified after Gilgamesh was conceived, then Gilgamesh is one-third mortal by default. It is a question that the poem does not raise. The poem's informing premise is that Gilgamesh's mortal portion renders the whole of him mortal.

•   •   •

As the poem proceeds, narrative pace and purpose alter. The story world opens out. The players test the boundaries of the map and break out into other realms, intersect with other times. The city stays at the centre: we depart from Uruk—and to Uruk we return. But it is a centre increasingly defined by its peripheries. They qualify it, and in turn they draw their meaning from it. When Gilgamesh and Enkidu return from the first adventure, the city solidifies around them once again. Its solidity is re-affirmed when Gilgamesh comes back at the poem's end and sends his companion the ferryman Ur-shanabi up onto the walls, to see what we shared at the start of the adventure. We observe now through altered eyes.

In the opening tablet of *Gilgamesh* the great walled city is experienced as a teeming community. There are men and women, and here the women take things into their own hands, petitioning their preferred gods to bring Gilgamesh under control. A surrounding countryside is lightly sketched, with trappers and shepherds, not too far away. The people know their king by sight, know the roads to the city, and are not afraid to enter it. Where does this peopled city with its peopled rural and wild environs go?

When the king and his friend set out on their quest for Humbaba, they are counselled by a chorus of elders. Enkidu gives a public speech (the tablet is too damaged to make much sense of it) and then the heroes are seen off by a crowd. Tablet 3 ends (in George):

The young men made *a fervent prayer* . . . :
    'Go, Gilgamesh, let . . . . . .
May your god go [before you!]
    May [Shamash] let you attain [your goal!]'
Gilgamesh and Enkidu *went forth* . . .

When the king and Enkidu return with their tribute of cedar wood and Humbaba's head and tusks for the city, the temples and the gods, in the tablets that survive no one welcomes them or marvels at the huge trunks, or the tusks. Attention has shifted in quite another direction. The action is between the protagonists and then between the protagonists and a fickle, sexual, vindictive goddess. What begins in a civic realm continues in a moral and religious realm. What starts with clamour and open conflict abandons the main stage to enter unfamiliar wilderness. When it returns it brings something of the wilderness with it, displacing the sense of people and political order.

Does the poetic material draw on quite separate, even disconnected, traditions? Or does the moral action of killing Humbaba have consequences not only for the protagonists but for the texture of the poem itself? *Gilgamesh* progresses from being chronicle, through adventure, to that adventure's moral and dramatic consequences, and then to lament. It refuses to conform to any single mode.

The sense of a peopled city (but a different one) returns in Tablet 11 when Uta-napishti tells his story of the Deluge and how he deceives his community—the people of Shuruppak—in order to get their assistance and to deflect their curiosity when he starts to build his boat. Ea urges him to get to work. He replies,

> "'I obey, O master, what thus you told me.
> I understood, and I shall do it,
> But how do I answer my city, the crowd and the elders?'"

He is to tell the people that Enlil, top god of Shuruppak, has contrived a hatred for him and he can no longer stay in Enlil's city. He must go and live with his protector, Ea, and Ea will reward the people of Shuruppak with food—birds, fish, great harvests. The metaphors Ea uses all have to do with floods: 'a shower of bread cakes', 'a torrent of wheat'. Uta-napishti gets the people to help him, in the expectation of reward. He feeds the workers well, and the boat becomes a communal project. When the time for the Deluge arrives, the hatch is sealed. The gods let loose the storm.

Like a battle [the cataclysm] passed over the people.
　One man could not discern another,
nor could people be recognised amid the destruction.

The gods themselves are terrified by the force of the storm: it
reduces them, and almost immediately they begin lamenting the
destruction they have made.

Even the gods took fright at the Deluge,
　they left and went up to the heaven of Anu,
lying like dogs curled up in the open.
　The goddess cried out like a woman in childbirth,
Belet-ili wailed, whose voice is so sweet . . .

And Belet-ili, who helped shape man in the first place, work-
ing with the god Enki, laments her part in the unmaking of her
creatures.

The goddess who cries out in this commotion 'like a woman in
childbirth' is Ishtar. We remember her romantic susceptibilities
and revenges. The Deluge reduces people to melted clay, the
gods to frightened dogs. Then, when, after the flood, Uta-napishti
starts burning incense in their honour, 'the gods gathered like
flies around the man making sacrifice'. Dogs, and, within forty-
odd lines, flies. Man may well have been punished at Enlil's be-
hest, but in his destruction the gods are reduced to bugs. The
metaphors are a form of *poetic* judgement. Man can only judge
the gods through language, in particular by means of apt meta-
phor. It is the gods' prerogative to judge and punish men in more
literal ways.

In Tablet 12, which lies beyond the formal end of our poem
but plays upon it, we are aware again of a human population,
but these men and a few women inhabit the Netherworld, where

they endure and (rarely) enjoy the aftermath of their mortal lives. The horror of the Standard Babylonian Netherworld is that the body remains, in some sense, a body, and suffering is expressed in physical terms, especially the suffering brought on by intense thirst, one of the worst conditions for people who live in parched lands. The Netherworld is remote from the noise and drama of Tablet 1 Uruk, where Gilgamesh is a young king testing the limits of his power and coming up against something like a popular will.

But we are getting more than a few tablets ahead of ourselves.

. . .

After butchering the Bull of Heaven, Gilgamesh and Enkidu wash their gory hands in the river Euphrates. They re-enter Uruk, clean hand in clean hand, and the citizenry stares at them as they go by in their chariot. There is no report of applause.

At the palace, Gilgamesh orders a celebration. Who, he asks, is the most handsome, the most male? His servant women oblige him with the reply, 'You are.' After revelry, the women and men fall asleep.

This time it is Enkidu's turn to see a dream. He wakes up to tell his dream to his friend.

TABLET 7

My friend

this is madness. You cannot blame the bend
in the river for an oxbow ambush. The gate
stands, it is ours, it is Uruk's. If fate
seems vicious, you must not be. Think the best,
never the worst. It is late. Try to rest.

Edwin Morgan, *The Play of Gilgamesh*

IT is tempting to regard the separate tablets as chapters or books
in their own right, deliberate units of poetry out of which the
larger poem is composed. Because they are so damaged at both
ends, we cannot say conclusively whether this is so, but the end
of Tablet 7 leads into the account of a dream. Elsewhere in the
poem the dream would follow without break from the announce-
ment that it has been seen. On the evidence of this low-key
transition, a tablet is an approximate measure of lines, not a for-
mal unit of narrative or verse: how much will fit, not how much
is formally appropriate.

What Enkidu dreams, in Standard Babylonian verse, has been
lost, but a prose summary in Hittite, presumably based on a Stan-
dard Babylonian original, survives. His dream sees the gods. They
have met in conclave. All the important ones are there: great

Anu, Enlil, Ea and Shamash. They want justice to be done to those responsible for slaying Humbaba. One of the perpetrators, Gilgamesh or Enkidu, should pay with his life. Enlil nominates Enkidu. Harsh words are exchanged, since Shamash favours Enkidu. In the end Enlil prevails and Enkidu is fingered.

When he tells this part of the dream, which is after all a reflection of things to come, Enkidu falls down at Gilgamesh's feet in a grief presaging their separation. Gilgamesh cannot put a positive spin on this dream. Enkidu's greatest sorrow is that he will lose the sight of his beloved brother.

(The Standard Babylonian verse text resumes at this point.)

Enkidu remembers the enormous cedar gate he has built and dedicated to Enlil, after the Humbaba expedition. He curses the gate as if he were addressing a person: it has not bought him sufficient favour—despite the effort that went into bringing the wood back and constructing it—to earn remission from death. The gate stands in for the god to whom it was dedicated. Intense blasphemy is at work, and Enkidu is not helping his case.

He should have devoted the gate to Shamash, who helped them, he says. He will destroy it. Gilgamesh listens and weeps. He warns his friend to avoid profanity, and promises to pray on his behalf and to offer the great gods valuable gifts if they will spare him. But Enkidu continues his complaint. He remembers the trapper who helped ensnare him, and curses him; and Shamhat the hierodule, who seduced him and set his friends the animals against him, alienating him from the natural life and drawing him into human society. Shamhat he curses at length and cruelly, as Gilgamesh cursed Ishtar before.

It is Shamash the Sun god, his champion, who answers him out of the sky, reminding him of his debts to Shamhat, how she humanised him and brought him to Uruk. Shamash urges Enkidu to change his tune: Shamhat brought him to Gilgamesh, and his beloved friend will see him off splendidly to the Netherworld, making the whole of Uruk mourn, and filling the gods of the Netherworld with respect for the new arrival.

Eventually Enkidu changes his tone. He turns to Shamhat and blesses her. Through the agency of Ishtar she will find a rich man who will unseat his wife, the mother of seven children, and set her in the wife's place. . . .

At this point a wonderful transformation has happened to Enkidu and something unusual has happened in poetry. The full humanising cycle of his life is complete. He has developed from a lump of clay to a child of nature, then into a social being, and, through learning to accept and to bless the woman who brought him out of the wild and into the presence of Gilgamesh, even despite the bleak fate through which he is passing, he develops into the more engaging brother, as it were. He becomes conscious of self and discovers a conscience. He can step outside his circumstances. On the brink of death, he reaches this point of moral maturity, well before his friend the king does. Gilgamesh has a long way yet to go before his growth equals Enkidu's.

Then Enkidu sees another dream, a terrifying one, in which death's emissary, another Thunderbird (as in Gilgamesh's fourth dream), binds him and bears him off to the Netherworld, and he witnesses (and, having been transformed into a dove, experiences physically) what it is like to be there. Eating dirt and clay and clothed in feathers are all those who have in their mortal years served the gods generously and faithfully. It is like a perversion of what the heroes see when they enter the cedar forest, the trees full of birds; there are the birds again, sinisterly reduced. And there is the Queen of the Netherworld Ereshkigal, and seated before her Belet-seri, reading aloud to her from a tablet. (This is one of the rare occasions when reading is portrayed.) Ereshkigal fixes her eye on Enkidu and asks him who he is. (The tablet is broken: What reply does he give? What happens next?)

When the story resumes, Enkidu is asking Gilgamesh to remember him, to remember what he has gone through. Gilgamesh calls it an unprecedented and unrepeatable dream, but we have yet to find the fragment of tablet to disclose it to us.

Now Enkidu is failing. He grows weaker. He dwindles for nine, ten, eleven days. On the twelfth he lies still and calls to his friend. Why could he not have died gloriously in battle? Then at least he would have been remembered. Again the text breaks off. His death throes have not been recovered, some thirty so far silent lines to bid his beloved Gilgamesh good-bye and perish.

TABLET 8

May the bear, the hyaena, the panther,
May the tiger, the stag, the leopard, the lion,
May the ox, the deer, the ibex—
May all the wild of the steppe
Weep for you!

Robert Temple, *He Who Saw Everything*

GILGAMESH mourns Enkidu long and loud. There is a lament tradition in Standard Babylonian literature, and Gilgamesh adds a striking chapter to it. He laments for seven nights and seven days. Knowing Enkidu's origins, he invites all the beasts of the wild to join him in the lamentation, from the gazelles in whose company we first saw him, to 'your father, the wild donkey', to the wild asses whose milk he drank. He wants the paths where Enkidu went to mourn him, and the elders and crowds of Uruk as well. And the mountains and grasslands. He enjoins the individual plants and trees to mourn. Then the wild animals, then the rivers. And finally, the people who have witnessed the great deeds the comrades have performed, from the shepherd boy to the harlot. Gilgamesh declares that he himself will wail 'like a hired mourner woman'. Then, 'He covered, like a bride, the face of his friend.' He pulled out his own hair by the roots. This eloquent desolation goes on powerfully for over fifty lines, longer than he spent cursing Ishtar.

Gilgamesh orders an opulent statue of his friend, opens his treasury and spends generously from it. He assembles the rich luggage Enkidu will take with him to the Netherworld to pay the gods down there. The tablets that itemise the treasures have been seriously damaged, the fore-edge entirely gone and with it half the words. Gilgamesh seems to be paying or paying off most of the gods of the Netherworld to secure the best and least painful passage for his friend. When the text resumes, Gilgamesh is assigning specific gifts to the many gods below. He knows all their names and callings—the butcher, the vizier, the scapegoat, the cleaner, the sweeper—and all will have their payment. (No wonder that, when Gilgamesh dies, though not in this poem, he is by some accounts made into a Netherworld god, in charge at death's threshold.)

Gilgamesh plans Enkidu's tomb. He throws a banquet where the catalogued grave goods are displayed to the invited people of Uruk. The tablet is broken at the end, and many lines are missing from it.

TABLET 9

Gilgamesh cried | not just for Enkidu.
Gilgamesh cried | for having to follow
Follow his friend | into the underworld
Never again | see the light of the sun.

Dust to dust | ashes to ashes
Gilgamesh searched | for Uta-napishtim
Uta-napishtim | the only survivor
The one who Enlil | saved from his Flood.

Jenny Lewis, *Gilgamesh Retold*

ENKIDU is dead and, amid his lamentations, suddenly Gilgamesh realises that he too will die. Death terrifies him. He knows what the Netherworld holds for all departed spirits. He sets out from his city in quest of the one man who has managed (with his wife, we later discover) to achieve deathlessness, Uta-napishti, son of Ubar-tutu and a prototype for Noah. His name means 'I found life' and he was long ago a living king of Shuruppak who was allowed to step free of time and live on undying. Gilgamesh wants to be like him.

He wanders into the wilderness, fighting, slaying and eating lions and dressing in their pelts. He becomes the Gilgamesh familiar from Babylonian art, lion-clad, dutifully digging wells.

Wells are for men to drink from, but they also spill water down into the Netherworld so the spirits of the dead can momentarily quench their thirst.

He wanders to the very ends of the earth. (There is a gap in the damaged tablet, supplied from an Old Babylonian tablet found in Sippar.) Shamash the Sun god worries about him and talks to him. Gilgamesh tells him he is absorbing as much light as he can because once dead in the Netherworld, darkness is forever. (Then Tablet 9 provides the text once more.) Here are the mountains where the Sun goes down and comes up.

To Mashu's twin mountains he came,
    which daily guard the rising [sun,]
whose tops [support] the fabric of heaven,
    whose base reaches down to the Netherworld.

For the first time we have a strong sense of a structure which encompasses the Netherworld, the world of the living, and the heavens. The whole is conceived in material terms and stretches the three dimensions, unfolding before our eyes the transcendent world through which Gilgamesh moves. There are few moments in which we sense an actual scene, but here the twin mountains that are deep rooted and rise into the heavens, while clearly emblematic, can also be visualised. A cosmic geography.

The scorpion men, grim guardians of the approach, block his passage beyond the mountains. They can stun with a glance, their 'radiance was fearful, overwhelming the mountain'. Gilgamesh covers his face, gathers his courage, and approaches. A scorpion man he addresses has a mate, and she tells him that he, Gilgamesh, is two-thirds god and one-third mortal. The king explains his mission, to get to his ancestor Uta-napishti, who lives at the ends of the world and is outside time. The scorpion man (who is more horrible conceptually than dramatically) poses no real threat to the king. The individual scorpion man he talks to tries to warn him off: no human being has ever gone through the pitch darkness of the Sun's tunnel under the mountains. Gilgamesh is as usual stubborn, persistent.

The scorpion man unbars the way and sends him forward with a kind of generous prayer and blessing. Gilgamesh passes through. He is fleet of foot and runs (the story counts the double hours) just fast enough to outstrip the Sun himself. At the far end of the tunnel, just before sunrise, he finds the trees of the gods, full of what look like fruit but are jewels. As he walks through the divine forest of stone, he is being watched.

TABLET 10

At the edge of the ocean, the tavern keeper
Shiduri was sitting. Her face was veiled,
her golden pot-stand and her brewing vat
stood at her side.

Stephen Mitchell, *Gilgamesh*

HE is watched by Shiduri as he walks along to the edge of the
sea beside which she lives. Shiduri is a curious tavern-keeper, a
crone with pots made of gold. She is extravagantly dressed, and
some scholars say she is an old goddess. As an inn-keeper, she
cannot have many customers among mortal men.

Gilgamesh approaches, clad in his lion skins. Grizzled and
travel-worn, he is a fearsome figure. She bolts the door and goes
to the flat roof of her tavern. We are reminded of how earlier
Ninsun went onto the roof of her house to enjoin Shamash to
look after her son and his friend on their quest to kill Humbaba.
Shiduri does not look up to the gods. She calls down, to know
the man's business.

He tells her the story of his exploits with Enkidu, following a
reverse chronology, from the Bull of Heaven to the Humbaba epi-
sode. How can this really be Gilgamesh, so wasted and hollow?
she asks. He tells his great sorrow, his long mourning, six days
and seven nights. He gave up the body of his friend when a

maggot fell from Enkidu's nostril. Gilgamesh began to fear for himself. Enkidu had turned to clay.

This is the first full description we have of the physical decay of Enkidu, the nostril maggot in particular, a key point when Gilgamesh retells the incident later, often, almost verbatim, on his journey. The detail may have appeared originally in Tablet 7, but the end of that tablet is so damaged we cannot be sure. As the text currently stands, the impression is that in Gilgamesh's memory the scene has clarified and the decay that accompanies death is finally registered.

Shiduri answers Gilgamesh wisely and at some length in an Old Babylonian poem that is believed to have come to us from the ruins of Sippar. These lines were not included in the 'standard' version of the poem that we generally read from, but they are worth hearing for the tonal and thematic elements they convey, a gently emollient tone that is muted in the Standard Babylonian *Gilgamesh*.

'O Gilgamesh, where are you wandering?

The life that you seek you never will find:
    when the gods created mankind,
death they dispensed to mankind,
    life they kept for themselves.

But you, Gilgamesh, let your belly be full,
    enjoy yourself always by day and by night!
Make merry each day,
    dance and play day and night!

Let your clothes be cleansed,
    let your head be washed, may you be bathed in water!

Gaze on the child who holds your hand,
    let a wife grow glad in your repeated embrace!

For such is the destiny [of mortal men,]
    that the one who is alive . . . . . .

Andrew George particularly notes the way in which here Shiduri uses the stative or passive voice. Acceptance will lead to the contentment a man can know on earth, the sense of a living present and the future that is embodied in the 'child' who is not, incidentally, gendered. The tablet gives out, and when the Standard Babylonian tablet resumes, Gilgamesh has ignored her advice. He is entirely focused on his quest.

He asks Shiduri to tell him the way to Uta-napishti. The journey is impossible, she says. Even so, like the scorpion man before, she tells him how to go—across the gulf, which includes at its centre the Waters of Death. Without delay he sets out to find the boatman Ur-shanabi, carrying his axe in one hand and his dirk in the other.

It takes him less time to get to Ur-shanabi, not the month and fifteen days as Shiduri predicted, because Gilgamesh, being Gilgamesh, is always fleet of foot. It is odd how on all the journeys that occur, the difficult trip out, with trials and challenges, does not entail a comparable return. This problem of continuity presents itself to modern readers but evidently not, in these terms, to the poem or its original readers and audience.

Gilgamesh, true to his nature, fights with the stone men that work with Ur-shanabi, destroying them. (We move to the Old Babylonian tablet to bridge a gap.) Ur-shanabi and Gilgamesh then introduce themselves to one another, a curious order of events. (Then Tablet 10 resumes.)

Gilgamesh repeats to Ur-shanabi his deeds with Enkidu and his sorrow. The story of the maggot recurs. He wants to go to Uta-napishti. But with his own hands, says Ur-shanabi, he has destroyed the very means of propulsion by destroying the stone men. If he wants to go, it's down to him: he must now make pine punting poles, immensely long and straight, to use in crossing the Waters of Death. Gilgamesh cuts and strips the pines. 'He trimmed them and furnished them each with a boss.' In terms of labour, this is his greatest challenge; while his more conventional adventures entailed courage and aggression, this requires solitary stamina. There is no Enkidu to share the labour with him.

Gilgamesh and Ur-shanabi punt across, and when the poles are used up Ur-shanabi takes off his shirt and Gilgamesh makes a sail of it. The wind propels them the rest of the way. Thus the Waters of Death are crossed in the usual time, three days.

Uta-napishti the Distant sees them coming and wonders why the stone men are broken. After the boat lands, Uta-napishti asks the same question that Ur-shanabi and Shiduri asked: why so wan and wasted? Again Gilgamesh tells of his exploits with Enkidu and repeats his lament, and again the maggot is seen to drop from Enkidu's nostril. He acknowledges that he fears endless death and that he has come to ask Uta-napishti the secret of his mortal survival, beyond time. The poem briefly changes key as Gilgamesh almost sings, in George's translation if not in Foster's or Dalley's, which have a much grimmer tone:

'Now let the gate of sorrow be barred,
   let [*its door be sealed*] with tar and pitch,
for my sake they shall [*interrupt*] the dancing no more,
   [for] me, happy and carefree . . .

The king remembers a time before sorrow; he has caused sorrow and will no longer do so. He wants to seal off any return to the misery of loss that has driven him to the ends of the world. The image of dancing comes from a register so far from the one the poem has been in up to now that its power is profoundly felt. After this brief shaft of light, the dark tone re-establishes itself.

Uta-napishti knows Gilgamesh's pedigree (being a god now, Uta-napishti must know many things before he needs to). He knows that Gilgamesh is made of divine and human substance. Why does he sorrow therefore? he inquires. He is a king and should be performing the duties of a king. He should compare his state with that of the pauper fool. His sorrow will accelerate his death. Death takes everyone, whatever they plan and do. The Anunnaki, the supreme gods, dispose, and there is no gainsaying them.

Dalley insists that 'we gain an overall impression of the free will of man which can fashion its own destiny and occasionally thwart the wishes of heaven'. Her argument is not convincing. Heaven has a cacophony of wishes, but the gods work out their problems through human agents. Men sometimes rebel, but this does not constitute free will, since their destinies are fixed. The 'predictive structure' is proof against individual volition. Uta-napishti's final speech on Tablet 10 could hardly be more categorical. It is also one of the most compelling passages in the poem, suddenly rich in metaphor and proverb. 'Man is snapped off like a reed in a cane-break,' George's Uta-napishti says, and Foster's, paratactic, simply phrased, each line a complete unit of sense, continues,

No one sees death,
No one sees the face of death,
No one [hears] the voice of death,

But cruel death cuts off mankind.

Do we build a house forever?

Do we make a home forever?

Do brothers divide an inheritance forever?

Do disputes prevail [in the land] forever?

Do rivers rise in flood for ever?

Dragonflies drift downstream on a river,

Their face staring at the sun,

Then, suddenly, there is nothing.

The sleeper and the dead, how alike they are!

They limn not death's image.

No one dead has ever greeted a human in this world . . .

We may want, at George's suggestion, to replace the dragon-fly with the mayfly, an even more vulnerable and ephemeral creature.

TABLET 11

the uroboros, as of Gilgamesh crossing the lake of pitch

& losing the secret of life to   (or of resin or gum arabic of

the water snake (among his   clothes the mother become
    woman

on the bank washing himself

of both the tar and the salt from the dive

to the bottom of the sea to get the plant

which is the secret which he wishes for

for all men, after the death—the stupid death,

by an irrelevance of attention—of

Enkidu

Charles Olson, 'Fragment of Translation and Comment' (12
December 1961)

OF all the tablets, Tablet 11 is the best preserved. No wonder
George Smith started with it—and fortunately, since it contains
the account of the Deluge that made him and the poem famous.

Gilgamesh, argumentative as always, tells Uta-napishti that he
contradicts himself. He stands incontestably present, a man of
flesh and blood no different from Gilgamesh himself, but one

who has managed to step beyond time and death. How, asks Gilgamesh, did he do this?

Uta-napishti tells his story.

He lived in the ancient city of Shuruppak on the Euphrates. It was a city where the gods had lived (as they do now in Uruk). The gods themselves resolved to drown the world. In Tablet 11 the cause is not specified, but in another Babylonian poem we are told that the god Enlil, ruler of earth and its people, was irritated by the ceaseless noise and bustle of mankind and wanted to put an end to it and recover peace and quiet.

The gods were sworn to secrecy, but Ea, a god much favoured in Shuruppak, who helped create man, found a way around the oath. He went to a fence made of reeds and spoke aloud to no one, but so that Uta-napishti, who is behind it, could overhear. In this manner he told Uta-napishti to build a great boat, leave everything behind except living things—animals, craftsmen and the like—and prepare for an inundation. He was to tell the citizens of Shuruppak that he was leaving them to live with Ea in the water world, promising his fellow citizens 'a rain of plenty'.

And so it came to pass. The craftsmen assembled and built the ship, huge and either square or round, depending on how you understand the measurements the poem provides. It had seven decks, each divided into nine compartments. The means of propulsion was punt poles. The workmen worked fast. The ship was completed in seven days.

Uta-napishti did not leave his wealth behind, as Ea had instructed, but instead bore it all on board, an impressive treasury. He took his whole family, too. The hatches were sealed, and on the morning when the flood commenced (the seven judges of the Netherworld lighted the land with their torches when the storm broke—lightning) the boat floated free of its moorings and out into the river. The river widened, the storm raged, the land was drowned. Bill Griffiths's resourceful and suggestive translation of this passage seeks to preserve the order and syntax of the original, so that the English reader can hear how, untransformed, the original language works. Uta-napishti speaks. Griffiths gives the line equivalents to the original text so we can follow.

80 whatever I-had, I laded
81 whatever I-had, I-laded (of) silver
82 whatever I-had, I-laded (of) gold
83 whatever I-had, I-laded (of) the seed of-living-things all
84 I brought on (board) ship all family-my and kin-my
85 cattleof-the-field, wild-creaturesof-the-field, the-sonsof-the-craftsmen all I-brought-in
86 a-fixed-time Shamash had-set
87 "when he-who-orders unease at evening will-shower-down a-rain of-riches/annihilating-force
88 "go on board the-ship; batten-up the-opening."
89 stated-time the arrived
90 when he-who-orders unease at evening showers-down a-rain of-riches/annihilating-force
91 the-day/weather to see fear I-had
92 the-weather to see fear I-had
93 I-went on board of-the-ship, battened-up the-entrance
94 for sealing the ship to Puzur-Amurri (the) boatman
95 the-vessel I-handed-over with contents-its
96 (when) something of-dawn (was) in view
97 came from the-edge of-the-heavens (a) cloud black
98 Adad in inside-it thunders
99 Nabu and Sharru went in front

100 went heralds (over) hill and plain
101 the-posts (of the world dam) Erragal tears-out
102 came Ninurta, the-dikes he-made-follow
103 The-Anunnaki lift-up torches
104 with glare-theirs setting-ablaze the-land
105 (concerning) him, Adad, consternation reaches the-sky
106 all light to blackness was-turned
107 (the wide) land like (a pot, shattered)
108 one day the-south-storm (blew)
109 gathering-speed as-it-blew, (submerging mountains)
110 like a-battle around (the people) it-overtakes (them)
111 not can-see any-man fellow-his
112 not can-be-distinguished people from the-sky
113 the-gods were-frightened-by the-deluge
114 they-shrank-back, they-went-up to the-heaven Of-the Anu (the highest)
115 gods like dogs cowered at-the-outer wall
116 cried-out Ishtar like a-woman-in-labour
117 moans-aloud the-Mistress of-the-gods, (a) loud noise:

The gods mourned for the death of their votaries and were themselves terrified by the Deluge they had made; they went up to the safe heaven of Anu and there lay down, in George, 'like dogs curled up in the open'. Their moral and physical scale is inverted. Great gods, creators and disposers of the fate of the world, are themselves subject and terrified by their handiwork.

Six days and seven nights the storm continued unabated. Then it stopped. 'The ocean grew calm, that had thrashed like a woman in labour,' a powerful image from an unexpected register. Slowly the water receded and fourteen islands emerged from the water-plain. The boat ran aground on the peak of Mount Nimush. On the seventh day Uta-napishti released a dove, which returned; then a swallow, which returned; then a raven, which found food and did not come back.

Uta-napishti made a sacrifice of incense to the gods (seven cauldrons, and then another seven) and they flocked to the scent like flies. The gods talked among themselves, playing the blame game. Enlil was responsible. Why, the others asked, did he not diminish mankind by means of a lion, a wolf, a famine, a plague: why a huge indiscriminate deluge destroying everything?

Enlil himself took wise Uta-napishti by the hand. He brought Uta-napishti's wife, too, and together they were blessed, transformed and removed from time. His fate, to remain man but survive like a god, was sealed, but he was removed from the ruins of his drowned city and from the vicinity of mankind, re-housed at the end of the world, where the rivers well up. It is a pale world without detail. It seems to the reader to be white on white, a world visited only by Ur-shanabi, and soon not even by him.

There will not be such another flood, says Uta-napishti; no comparable occasion will arise to cause the gods to set Gilgamesh outside time.

But if Gilgamesh can stay awake for six days and seven nights, defeating Sleep, he may have a chance of overcoming Death. Gilgamesh accepts the challenge. As soon as he starts trying to stay awake, however, he falls into a deep slumber. Uta-napishti's wife bakes a loaf of bread every day, and marks the wall. When at last Gilgamesh rouses, after seven nights, he insists that only a moment has passed. But the dry and stale loaves and the marks on the wall tell against him. He realises that what seemed a snatched slumber was in fact seven nights of deep sleep. He has failed.

Uta-napishti dismisses Ur-shanabi from his service for his disobedience in ferrying a mortal across the Waters of Death. He instructs him to help Gilgamesh bathe. Then Uta-napishti clothes

Gilgamesh in kingly raiment, raiment that will stay fresh and new until he gets back to Uruk, to resume his royal duties.

Inevitably, another question to do with narrative continuity arises. This one seems important because of what it tells us about the structure of the poem. If Uta-Napishti is outside time, and aeons before was taken to the end of the world by Ur-shanabi, who still lives and still runs the boat service, is Ur-shanabi equally deathless? Or was he only outside time so long as he fulfilled his duties obediently? Or are the roles timeless (like kingship) and the men who fill them transients (like Gilgamesh)?

· · ·

Now Gilgamesh has a new companion, the boatman, and together they cross back over the Waters of Death, but not before Uta-napishti's wife, who has waited quietly in the background, speaks up, hospitably urging her husband to give the king a parting gift. The gift is another secret, a secret that will restore a man's youth. In the seabed beneath the Waters of Death grows a prickly plant that rejuvenates. If Gilgamesh can recover this he can revive and extend his life. Uta-napishti gives him instructions on where to dive and find it.

As they cross the Waters of Death, Gilgamesh finds the right spot, weights himself with stones, plunges with a hero's strength and courage to the seabed, and retrieves the miraculous 'Plant of Heartbeat', as he calls it. He will try it out on an old man in Uruk to see if it works, and if it does he will apply it to himself and call it 'Old Man Grown Young'. It reminds us that the meaning of Bilgames, the Old Babylonian form of Gilgamesh's name, is 'The Ancestor is a Hero'.

On the way to Uruk-the-Sheepfold the king and the boatman stop at a pool to bathe. Gilgamesh leaves his untried miraculous plant with his fine robes by the pool. A serpent slides into his clothes, eats the plant and slithers away renewed, shedding its old skin. Here is proof that the herb works: but the herb is also lost forever and, with it, Gilgamesh's last hope of cheating Death.

Gilgamesh's journey to Uta-napishti's is an enormous series of challenges and a long trek. His return entails none of the original trials: no Shiduri, no race with the Sun under the mountain, no scorpion men. As before, the trial belongs to the outward journey and the way back is unproblematic. It goes by—apart from the treacherous snake—in a flash. The geography of the poem, in terms of perils and challenges, is a one-way system.

Ur-shanabi and Gilgamesh arrive in Uruk. There is again no welcoming crowd. What had at the beginning of the poem been a busy place feels like a ghost town at the king's return. Of course he has not come back in triumph, as when he arrived with Humbaba's head and the cedar trees, but in defeat. The conclusion of the poem focuses on the king and his new companion Ur-shanabi, the forcibly retired boatman of the Standard Babylonian Noah, Uta-napishti. Gilgamesh (repeating the opening lines) sends Ur-shanabi up to the battlements to admire the city he has fortified. Seven wise men laid its foundations. How large it is, with the date grove, the clay-pit, the temple of Ishtar, 'three square miles and a half is Uruk's expanse.'

The poem ends with a brief map-inventory—the same we were provided at the outset—and a set of measurements.

TABLET 12

IT would have been a happy coincidence if *Gilgamesh* had had twelve integrated books, like the *Aeneid*, half the number of the *Iliad* and the *Odyssey*. But the tablets we have are more a series of long, damaged pages than books in their own right.

Portions of Tablet 12, however, connect in suggestive ways to some of the *Gilgamesh* themes. The tablet includes a partial translation of an Old Babylonian poem in the latter part of which Enkidu is brought back from the Netherworld for a visit with Gilgamesh. He has gone to the Netherworld to recover items belonging to Bilgames—wooden toys, his *ellag* and his *ekidma*, ball and mallet. The king has made himself a nuisance playing with them, and forcing the young men of Uruk to play, too, as before he had wrestled with them. This ball-and-mallet game sounds like an early form of croquet, though it was probably less polite.* Eventually both *ellag* and *ekidma* 'fall through' into the Netherworld, a great relief to Uruk, one can imagine, but not to Bilgames, who wants them back. Enkidu agrees to retrieve them. Bilgames gives him strict instructions on what to do and what not to do in the Netherworld. Enkidu disobeys all the instructions, one by one, and the Netherworld seizes him.

Bilgames goes to Enlil and begs him to help. Enlil refuses to speak. The moon god does not respond. Enki (the Old Babylonian name of Ea, god of the water table) agrees to help, asking

---

* Other versions speak of a *pukku* and a *mikku,* which Samuel Kramer takes to be a drum and drumstick, and it is this version that affected Charles Olson.

Shamash the Sun in one version, and a young warrior in another, to bring up Enkidu's shade to speak with Bilgames, an early prototype for Orpheus and Eurydice.

Up comes the shade. The friends are briefly, miserably, reunited. Bilgames asks questions and Enkidu replies, mainly about the circumstances of the people he has seen in the Netherworld. But the passage that has attracted considerable attention in recent years is the one that seems to confirm the sexual character of Gilgamesh and Enkidu's relations, at least in the original poem. When they meet they hug and kiss, as they have done before. Enkidu laments. Benjamin Foster's Enkidu is impassioned but circumspect. He says:

> My body you once touched, in which you rejoiced,
> It will [never] come [back].
> It is infested with lice, like an old garment,
> It is filled with dust, like a crack (in parched ground).

In Andrew George's translation of one of the surviving tablets, Enkidu is more graphic, modulating to gothic, about their touching and then about his own process of physical decomposition.

> '[*My friend, the*] *penis* that you touched so your heart rejoiced,
>   a grub devours [(it) . . . like an] old *garment.*
> [*My friend, the crotch* that you] touched so your heart rejoiced,
>   it is filled with dust [like a crack in the ground.]'

At this news Gilgamesh throws himself on the ground, according to George, in overwhelming grief. The poem repeats the grief line. Or (Foster), working on a different tablet: '"Woe is me!" cried the lord, and sat down in the dust.'

Then he calms down and returns to interrogating Enkidu systematically, about the types he has seen in the Netherworld. They are categories of people rather than individuals, and what is of interest is their relative comfort and relative position in the Netherworld, established in relation to the number of sons they have or have not left behind. He asks about men who have died and left behind one, two, three . . . up to seven sons. Each is more blessed than the one before, because sons make provision and sacrifice to the gods of the Netherworld, ensuring the comfort of their forebears. The man with seven sons is very nearly a god. But the childless man, like the palace eunuch, is of less than no account. Those whose ghosts have no provider fare ill in the Netherworld. Those who die early, before reaching adulthood, are made comfortable. As for women, Enkidu's testimony includes very few of them ('the woman who never gave birth' and the unmarried woman), or their daughters.

Gilgamesh asks after his own mother and father, who are suddenly not divine but mortal. Foster translates:

'Did you see my mother and my father, wherever they
    dwelt there?'
'I saw them.'
'How do they fare?'
'The two of them drink filthy water at the field of
    carnage.'

Gilgamesh returns to Uruk, to his palace. He makes vows to relieve his parents' posthumous suffering.

• • •

George is not convinced that Tablet 12 belongs to his version of the poem. While the first eleven tablets are a poem in their own right, the material in Tablet 12, translated from known Old Babylonian originals, is tacked on because of the names of the protagonists. Enkidu, safely dead and mourned, is conjured back, undoing the theme of loss and fear of death. He is not entirely lost, and he is not quite dead. (It might be argued that his return as an emanation, an immaterial ghost, intensifies Gilgamesh's sense of loss, but such a view is rather too novelistic; and Gilgamesh's grief is soon displaced by curiosity about the Netherworld itself.)

The Netherworld content most relevant to the main story could have been integrated, more or less, into Tablet 7, when Enkidu sees his dream, or has his vision, of the underworld. For George the first eleven tablets form a kind of symmetry: 5 – 1 – 5. Tablet 12 is unmetrical, prosaic. It spoils his pattern, which he believes reflects Sin-leqi-unninni's own plan for the poem, when he brought the parts into the uncertain, porous whole much of which we enjoy today. Sin-leqi-unninni is waiting for us a little way ahead.

IMAGINING *GILGAMESH*

MANY contemporary English versions of *Gilgamesh* by poets apply familiar templates to a remote, knotty original. This is what N. K. Sandars does in *The Epic of Gilgamesh*. She works the poem into prose; most contemporary poet-translators attempt some kind of verse. They all teach *Gilgamesh* some of the manners of their time and culture, resolve symbol in metaphor or image, add detail and even incident, and conceal the cracks in the original tablets.

They tell a not so discretely modernised version of the story. The poet Jeffrey Wainwright says of the popular verse translation by Stephen Mitchell (2004) that it 'reads very fluently to me, though it might work too hard to make [the poem] familiar to a present-day readership'. It is a bit too familiar for the poet and critic Carol Rumens, who recalls, 'I didn't like it, on the whole. I hate male Hero stories: the big axes, the (implied) big penises and the big egos: a big turn-off.' One wants to say, 'But that *isn't* the poem', and yet it is Mitchell's take on the poem. 'I filed *Gilgamesh* mentally,' Rumens declares, 'with books I didn't really want to read, struggled with, and was glad to finish.'

Stephen Mitchell tells us that he drew his version from literal translations by scholars and from other verse and prose renditions. Nine of them provided his orientation points. As he skittered back and forth between them, 'I felt rather like a bat, feeling out the contours of the original text by flinging sound waves into the dark.' It is a wonderful and candid image of the linguistically sightless translator finding his way.

Candid, too, is the statement that follows: 'Once my prose version was completed, I began the real work, of raising the language to the level of English verse.' This is not a conventional approach to translation or—indeed—to making poetry. The idea that poetry is the result of pumping up prose—pumping it beyond the tension of mere verse to something really tight and bouncy—seems to emanate from those schools of creative writing in which heightened texture and effect are the declared goals. James Fenton, reviewing Mitchell's version in the *Guardian*, 'immediately went out and bought two other versions' because he found it readable but it did not 'read quite like an ancient poem, let alone like a very ancient poem indeed'. What Mitchell regarded as—in his words—'quirks of Akkadian [Standard Babylonian] style' and did away with, lest we find them tedious, in particular the 'word-for-word repetitions of entire passages', Fenton correctly speculates 'might be not quirks but characteristic features of primitive poetry'.

When we have read the poem attentively in a scholarly edition, we might take issue with Fenton's use of the word 'primitive', but with him we will demur when Mitchell stresses how 'he has changed images that were unclear, added lines, cut fragmentary passages and occasionally reordered them'. The original for him is a pretext, an occasion for his own speculative inventions. He is more up front than Sandars; but in a way, given the tremendous scholarship that has accrued since Sandars undertook her ground-breaking popularisation, he is also more culpable of assimilating the original into his own over-confident culture, his rather too lenient poetics.

Fenton notes in Mitchell's introduction 'an unwelcome desire to inject relevance into the epic, with talk of crusades and jihads, of superpowers and "polarised fundamentalisms". I would much rather approach a 4,000-year-old poem without making such crude demands for political payback.' It is a note that jars not only in Mitchell's version but in other contemporary translations and advocacies of the work. *Gilgamesh*'s otherness is not going to reward modern readers, or modern writers, with what it tells us about ISIS or American foreign policy. If we avoid burdening the poem with our current concerns, we may be able to approach it in a disinterested but informed spirit, even if we are ignorant of Old Babylonian, Standard Babylonian and the other languages in which *Gilgamesh* fragmentarily survives.

Or we might commit to an extreme approach, which insists on looking at the fragmented poem through the fragmentation of contemporary history. At the time of the Gulf War, said the American poet Andrea Brady, 'everyone was doing *Gilgamesh*'. The Penguin edition of Andrew George's scholarly version, designed for general readers, appeared in 1999. It was acknowledged with a long letter by the poet J. H. Prynne, published by Brady in the magazine *QUID*, and it was widely read and adopted as a formal and thematic resource. Brady herself set to work on a poem to be entitled 'Sweatbox', described by the poet Harry Gilonis as 'a Gulf-War-related reworking of *Gilgamesh*'. It was abandoned, but she spoke intriguingly about it:

> That text attempted to plot the *Gilgamesh* epic, tablet by tablet, against the daily war (the second invasion of Iraq). Epic fragments were transported by Penguin Classics to a nook in London then out back to a pixellated field sewn with cluster bomblets and the shards of the Nemean lion. I busied myself at the British Museum, reading the blurbs, constellating fragments as a melancholic formal reminder of the fractures and losses in real-time reporting and in the dispersal of a living culture. But I couldn't keep up with the news, couldn't fit that fast degeneration to an epic impasto

worth thousands of years. My appropriations showed through: the desire for wholeness implicit in the phrases airlifted from news bulletins; the desire for the right and the position to speak, for consensus and legitimacy of representation. The absence of those rights and places, the mourning echoes of the epic voice, turned the poem all tawdry ironic—better than a barbaric silence, but only just.

This grave and penetrating piece of self-analytical truthtelling, written out of the poet's lived engagement, might stand as an example to any would-be translator of what a poet's responsibility should be to a poem as multifarious and unresolved as *Gilgamesh*, and to her own time.

. . .

The composite textual nature of *Gilgamesh*—rebuilt from many fragments taken from various languages and periods—and its instability, the fact that tomorrow a new fragment or a whole new tablet might emerge and alter our perception of the work, provide a license to some non-scholarly translators less ethically alert than Andrea Brady. They do not feel compelled to be faithful to a single version or to respect the formal and thematic qualities of the original, even in the state in which it has reached us. Why be faithful at all? Editors like George draw material from versions and fragments composed millennia apart and in different languages: Old Babylonian, Standard Babylonian and Hittite may share characters and incidents, but the characters themselves are differently drawn in different cultures, at different times. Why shouldn't translators enjoy comparable liberties?

But scholars give due notice of interpolation and speculation. Enkidu the servant in the Sumerian version, where he has no backstory, becomes Gilgamesh's peer in the Standard Babylonian, with his origins sketched in. A scholar will borrow from the early poem when material from the later tablets is missing, but there is seldom a question of replacing later elements with earlier in the cases where both survive. The death of Enkidu in our Standard Babylonian version has much in common with the death of Bilgames in the Old Babylonian poem. Andrew George notes that the two deaths 'share a literary pattern'.

Time and history have done enough to mar the record. When English poet-translators over-ride the discriminations of scholarship in the presumed interests of their readership and market, they further blur and erase as they go. For the poet, editor and translator Rod Mengham, '*Gilgamesh* remains as the prime example of cultural untranslatability'. For that reason literary translators without the original languages do well to steer clear and leave the poem to the experts.

Gabriel Josipovici, as a Bible scholar, found the poem fascinating, 'but somehow it's never quite entered my "sphere". I did when writing my Bible book [*The Book of God*, 1988] read up the scholarship. [. . .] But it never, for some reason (the translations?), touched me the way Homer has.' It is still waiting for its definitive translator.

German has been more fortunate. As early as 1916, the great German poet Rainer Maria Rilke read a new, free, Sandars-like rendition of *Gilgamesh* by Georg Burckhardt, brought out by the publisher of his own books. He went back from this new adaptation to an older, more literal version from 1911 by Arthur Ungnad, *Das Gilgamesch-Epos*. Rilke's response is prominently quoted and even cited as an epigraph in Anglophone studies of *Gilgamesh*. Writing to his publisher's wife, Rilke called the experience of reading *Gilgamesh* 'ungeheuer' or 'stupendous', 'the greatest thing that can happen to a person'. It is 'das Epos der Todesfurcht', the epic of the fear of death. She wrote back suggesting that he might undertake a revision of Burckhardt's version, of which he did not unreservedly approve. He declined, saying that the poem was for reciting, not reading on the page: he had entertained his daughter Ruth (who must have been in her mid-teens at the time) with it. After his initial encomium, one looks almost in vain for further references to the poem in Rilke's correspondence. Around the same time as the first letter, he wrote to another of his female correspondents telling her he would like to recite the poem to her. He does not urge her to read it to herself. He does comment on the gaps in the text that elicit the reader's involvement.

How much impact did the poem have on him and his poetry? Or, after his first excited response, did he leave it behind? The poet and essayist Iain Bamforth combed through Rilke's correspondence looking for more evidence. The *Chronik seines Lebens und seines Werkes*, a time line, 'edited most recently by Ingeborg Schnack (Insel, 2009), which gives a blow-by-blow account of everything Rilke did through the years,' Bamforth writes, 'has a very detailed index, and there's only one single mention of Gilgamesh, for that fatidic month of Dec 1916. Nothing else.' By 1917 *Gilgamesh* seems to have been water under Rilke's bridge.

The Dante and Rilke scholar Patrick Boyde, who semi-staged *Gilgamesh and Enkidu* at Cambridge in 2010, gave an as yet unpublished paper in April 2010 in which he looked not at the letters or biographical data but at eighty lines from the tenth *Duino Elegy* of 1922, juxtaposing it with an excerpt from the Ungnad translation. Among his suggestive conclusions, he writes:

> If you set out from Rilke's *poetry* (rather than from the two little-known letters), you will be encouraged to keep looking at the universal themes of Suffering and Fear of Death,

of Friendship and Courage, of Quests for Meaning. You will remember that some 'Leiden' are 'Ur-Leiden' (with the connotation that they are not just ancient, but stem/core/ vital, and that they will never be outmoded). In other words, you'll remember that every individual—even a philologist—must face physical pain and mental suffering in his or her own life, must endure bereavement, should prepare to die, should come to understand that suffering and mourning are an integral part of life, 'unser wintewähriges Laub'.

Rilke's poetry can help you to see that Sîn-leqi-unninni [. . .] is a *poeta theologus* (which is what Aristotle called Empedocles, and what the fourteenth century called Dante), and that his poems could still play a vital part in education.

Whatever impression *Gilgamesh* left on Rilke, what he said about it in the first rush of enthusiasm had a lasting impact on the marketing and transmission of the poem. It was its spinnaker.

Bamforth did suggest a valuable alternative witness to Rilke, the Nobel laureate Elias Canetti, who 'talks about the impact of Gilgamesh in his autobiography, and I found this interesting comment in his collection of notes *Die Fliegenpein*: "Gilgamesh is no less compelling than the Bible. It has *one* advantage over the latter: a hostile goddess against whom its protagonist is openly in combat. Femaleness, however it is interpreted, is *present*. In the Bible the presence is merely a diminished one: Eve."' Canetti remembered public performances of *Gilgamesh* during his youth: it was part and parcel, for him, of living memory. But his testimony is too nuanced to lend itself to the poem's marketing.

Alison Brackenbury, the English writer, reminded me of another German affected by *Gilgamesh*, the East German poet Peter Huchel. In 'Der Holunder öffnet die Monde' ('The Elder Tree opens its moons') he writes, in Michael Hamburger's translation,

Son,
little son Enkidu,
you left your mother, the gazelle,
your father, the wild donkey,
to go with the whore of Uruk.
The milk-bearing goats fled.
The steppe withered.

Behind the city gate
with its seven iron bolts
you were instructed by Gilgamesh,
who crosses the frontier between heaven and earth,
to slash the ropes of death.

Darkly noon burned on the brickworks,
darkly the gold lay in the king's room.
Turn back, Enkidu.
What did Gilgamesh give you?
The gazelle's lovely head submerged.
Dust beat your bones.

'I shared Peter Huchel's preoccupation with Enkidu,' says Brackenbury, developing a reading which in effect greens the poem in ways I find convincing, because the nature/nurture contest now has a rather different aspect from the one it did when *Gilgamesh* began to matter to Anglophone writers. Brackenbury continues in her letter to me,

I identified with it still more strongly as workable blue-
prints for wind and solar power languished in filing cabi-
nets, as world temperatures rose, on graph after graph—
and a reviewer in a leading literary journal asked, with
commendable frankness, if there was any point in writing
a poem about a bird. If you live too long in Uruk, all you
have left is the gold crammed into the King's room. Can you
breathe, eat, or even dream of that? The great can inspire
the small. [. . .] I now realise that Huchel was in his sev-
enties when he distilled *Gilgamesh* into a few lines. I believe
that Edwin Morgan, too, was in his seventies when he
drafted his *Play of Gilgamesh*. This poem is a country for
both young and old. Do older writers see it with particular
clarity?

Brackenbury's question is hard to answer, but it is the case
that the scholar-translator Andrew George revisits the poem on
what must be almost a daily basis. He knows it so well that points
in it clarify in his mind as he goes. It is a living text, and living
alongside it his versioning matures. I anticipate an overhaul of
his original translation that, while keeping faith with it, will
bring it into clearer and more precise relief.

The poet Nina Bogin knows the poem from French transla-
tions, and her relationship with it is on the face of it more the-
matic than formal, given her own concerns and the versions in
which she encountered it:

I was, and continue to be, impressed both by the strange-
ness of the epic (the characters, the events) and at the same
time by the familiarity of its themes—combat, war, depar-
ture and the traversing of seemingly insurmountable obsta-
cles, forests, monsters, return, death and the longing for
immortality. But no doubt what struck me most was its

almost 'modern' *psychology*, if that is the right term. The friendship or comradeship between the King Uruk and Enkidu seems, once again, both strange and familiar. Strange because, since women play a very small role in this epic, the intense love-relationship is between two male figures, Uruk and Enkidu. Familiar because the theme is eternal: the intensity of love, the refusal to accept the death of the loved one, and finally, acceptance. At least one other important theme is that of the emblematic city-state, its architecture— buildings and ramparts; its citizens, and the desire for immortality through a lasting architectural monument.

Gilgamesh remains vulnerable. It clearly affects readers and writers; it is also impacted upon, commandeered, re-read and misread. It has suffered the fate of long-established classical text, but—being a newcomer—it has suffered in a more accelerated form: it has been annexed and academicised, put upon, traduced, or—we might rather say—colonised, in a post-modern spirit. The contemporary literary world is crawling with cultural police who condemn in creative contexts precisely these kinds of 'misuse' of otherness. They haven't yet brought *Gilgamesh* within their protective ring. Assumptions about *Gilgamesh*'s origins, its audience, its nature and meaning, are made casually, wilfully, by eager translators working from other translations and traditions.

In 2006 the American poet Yusef Komunyakaa with the director Chad Gracia adapted the poem—with actors and chorus— into a Greek tragic form, subtitling it *A Verse Play*. It is a convincing transposition, but remote from *Gilgamesh*. Scholars, too, can be culpable, assigning the poem to an inappropriate genre, assuming without convincing evidence its origins in oral traditions, and so on.

Almost invariably, critics who read Gilgamesh as epic are disappointed with it. Thorkild Jacobsen, writing in 1946, sets the tune. As an epic it 'does not come to an harmonious end; the emotions which rage in it are not assuaged; nor is there, as in tragedy, any sense of catharsis, any fundamental acceptance of the inevitable. It is a jeering, unhappy, unsatisfactory ending. An inner turmoil is left to rage on, a vital question finds no answer.' We might agree that the ending is unsatisfactory, the repetition of the opening creating a symmetry which is aesthetically misjudged, whatever the intended pattern. But the other terms in Jacobsen's conclusion are anachronistic. We might ask, who is doing the jeering—an assumed narrator? And might not the vital question find its answer (however unsatisfactory the aesthetics of the case) in the twelfth tablet, which specifically asks and answers questions about the Netherworld: if Gilgamesh has to die, what will death be like? The poem's final failure as an epic may be due to the fact that it isn't an epic, and that Sin-leqi-unninni's transformation of traditional material into something like the poem we have today was not an exercise in genre.

Sandars calls the poem *The Epic of Gilgamesh* on the authority of earlier scholars. She goes so far as to suggest that the *Iliad* might have been recited at Nineveh. The suggestion that a Greek might have heard Gilgamesh or a king in Nineveh might have heard the *Iliad* is no less or more plausible than that Shakespeare might have read *Don Quixote* in the years of his retirement in Stratford-on-Avon: the dates work, but—so what? The most we can hope is that, if he did, he enjoyed it. The Austrian poet-translator Raoul Schrott suggests that Homer himself came from Mesopotamia to Greece and there are therefore deep-rooted connections between the traditions. Implausible, the scholars say. Or irrelevant.

Even so, most writers today insist that *Gilgamesh* is an epic and, what is more, the fruit of an oral tradition. They assume it was composed for performance before an audience. Dalley says it was 'very probable' that the Old Babylonian poems out of which it grew were 'for entertainment' in courts, private houses, 'around the camp fires of desert caravans, or on the long sea voyages. . . .' She suggests that the written poem was kept fresh, aerated as it were, by oral traditions that persisted alongside it. Given the number of tablets and fragments so far found, if there was solid evidence for orality, it might have been established by now. We ask for evidence, not because these assumptions are self-evidently wrong, but because they are not and cannot at this stage be proven: they are not self-evidently *right*.

Gilgamesh resists them. Its *otherness* is what unprogrammed readers find gripping, its inassimilable netherworldness. The New Zealand poet John Gallas exclaims, 'what lingers and goes to my soul, and gets used, is that Hot-Light, completely different (time and place) world—a bit like seeing a film from Siberia or Kazakhstan where you goggle at trees and houses and clothes and weather and the way people behave because you know nothing about that period and/or society.' What imperils the poem are fashions of classical and modern criticism and the determined single-mindedness of critics. Is it possible to work out the poem's own terms and learn to read it in the ways (plural, given its long life in adjacent and consecutive cultures) that it asks to be read?

We should remain alert for the distorting filters that critics—often without realising they are doing so—keep placing between us and *Gilgamesh*. It can be as though we had gone trustingly to the oculist who, fitting us for spectacles, keeps putting into the slots inappropriate lenses and telling us we can see more clearly with them. In a sense we can, but we are not seeing what is there. And we *are* seeing what is not really there.

• • •

What is there? Where do we begin?

Gilgamesh is unique. All poems are unique, but *Gilgamesh* is more unique than most.

First, the poem does not have an author, a fact to which we will return.

And then, we should not regard it as a poem in the singular. It is not a stable or settled text but a changing, growing and contested construction made out of wholes or fragments of inscribed clay tablets in several languages, brought together, matched, collated. It is an edited work whose apparent solidity gives way as soon as we get up close and press, curiously, for the most basic sense.

For example, we know the proposed measurements of the boat that Uta-napishti builds at the behest of Ea, his patron and the god of the water table, in Tablet 11:

'The boat you will build
  her dimensions all shall be equal:
her length and breadth shall be the same,
  cover her with a roof, like the Ocean Below.'

Andrew George's translation of Uta-napishti's narrative leaves the reader alert to the ambiguities in the language. N. K. Sandars in her prose version says, 'let her beam equal her length'. Stephanie Dalley, with the benefit of knowing the language, is less categorical: 'Her width and length shall be in harmony'.

'By the fifth day I had set her hull in position,
　　one acre was her area, ten rods the height of her sides.
　At ten rods also, the sides of her roof were each the same
　　　length.
　　I set in place her body, I drew up her design.'

George outlines the inner disposition of space, but not a shape
is in sight. Because the division of compartments on the seven
decks is into nines, a regular square might seem logical, divided
into 3×3. Edwin Morgan in his dramatisation of *Gilgamesh* makes
it 'high and square like an ocean ziggurat'. Sandars has, 'On the
fifth day I laid the keel and the ribs, then made fast the plank-
ing.' It is a conventional-seeming ship-building scene. But she
adds, 'The ground-space was one acre, each side of the deck mea-
sured one hundred and twenty cubits, making a square.' But
when it finally floats it has a conventional tiller. For the scholar
Gunnar Olsson the boat is a huge cube with 63 compartments.
He dubs it a *thesaurus sapientiae*.

Or is it round, as has been argued, and even demonstrated ex-
perimentally, by the irresistibly inventive Assyriologist Irving
Finkel? He had a to-scale version of what he believed to be Uta-
napishti's boat plans constructed and sailed. Or is it a more stan-
dard ship shape? The poem gives us statistics concerning caulk-
ing with pitch and loading the human, animal and material cargo,
but still no clarification of what the construction looks like. Are
we in the region of paradox—not of Theseus's ship (if every plank
of the original ship is replaced, in what sense is it still the origi-
nal ship) but of Uta-napishti's floating structure (if all the ele-
ments of which the ship is made are the same, but the shape
changes, is it the same ark)?

The Babylonian word for periphery is sometimes translated
as 'circumference'. In English, 'circumference' has 'circ' in it,

suggesting a circle, but the meaning has changed and come to apply to the maximum outer measurement of a geometric form. 'One acre was her circumference,' writes Dalley, mixing a space with a length measurement and thus, with a blur, avoiding the need to choose a shape. The circularity inherent in Latin is not in the Standard Babylonian. The Standard Babylonian word does not necessarily entail even a curve. The way the poem records the *measurements* makes the construction sound like a large square. Benjamin Foster speaks of it as an 'enormous cube'.

My imagination favours a round or oval ship, but my reading of the translation of the most dependable evolving text, George's, inclines me to the—on the face of it—more improbable Rubik ark. The text provides information, but at the same time withholds what could bring that information into visual focus.

Cuneiform, devised to make inventories and lists in the languages that adopted it, is specific when it comes to size, distance, weight. It is good to know how much gold and grain Uta-napishti loads on board, and how he stows it: more important than to know what the ship, a mere vehicle to see him through the seven nights of the Flood, looks like. The poem is true to its culture, and a translation that perceives and respects this truth naturally, in following it, foreignises the English text so that readers sense and respond to the unfamiliar character of the presentation. The poem stops short of giving us an image. The translator should consider doing likewise. We have the bill of lading, which is what matters. This foregrounding of value over visibility recurs, even in the descriptions of figures and actions. If it does not occur to the poem that a resolved image matters, can we try to read in such a way that it does not matter to us, either? That way we might get closer to the sensibility of the poem.

Similarly, as noted earlier, when we are directed onto the wall of Uruk to admire the view, we are told to see 'a square mile of city, a square mile of date palms, a square mile of clay-pit, and half a square mile of Ishtar's temple'. Three and a half squares. Nothing actually to visualise, but a sense of rich matter contained. With such a map, we won't get very far when we come down off the walls and start to walk around the city.

GETTING A GRIP

GILGAMESH is decidedly remote from our world and time. Uruk, the Mesopotamian city near the fertile banks of the Euphrates, where the poem's action begins and ends, is one of the earliest cities in the world. Its citizens and their king live in close proximity to one another. Few barriers separate them, so that a trapper from the countryside can gain immediate audience with the king, and the king knows the temple harlots by name. The shepherds who tend their flocks three days away from Uruk, providing the city with food and wool, know their king and talk about him familiarly. At the time of the poem, Old Babylonian Uruk had between 50,000 and 80,000 inhabitants and was probably one of the biggest cities in the world. It declined after 2000 BCE, but some insist (through a very doubtful etymology) that it gave its name, through Arabic, to the country we now know as Iraq.

It is alien, it is strange, an urban setting presented as if for the first time. Can we visualise it precisely from the detail we are given, or does the problem we encountered with the ship and the heroes' stature recur? Are the passages we read intended as descriptions in our sense, or do they carry meaning in a different way, less to the eye than to another faculty, agreed and shared by those to whom the poem was originally addressed?

And whom *did* it address? There are as many enigmas as face the walrus and the carpenter walking along the beach in Lewis Carroll's poem. Definitive answers come there none. Thinking about the ways in which *Gilgamesh* was composed, or how it evolved, how it was preserved and rediscovered, extends our sense of reading and writing, language and translation, poetic shapes and forms. But it doesn't resolve in a set of definitive answers.

We are not dealing with a single world and time. We are not dealing with a single language. *Gilgamesh* starts as a series of discrete Old Babylonian stories about Bilgames composed as early as 2250 BCE, but well after the historical king Gilgamesh went to the Netherworld. The earliest surviving versions of these stories were pressed by scribes into soft damp river clay tablets with a cut reed stylus. The clay tablets dried, hardened and were preserved and valued. Important texts (laws, omens, chronicles) were copied and re-copied, used as exercises in the scribal schools whose debris is a crucial scholarly resource, and collected into libraries. Fragments of the poems have been found as far afield as Anatolia in modern Turkey. The poet John Wilkinson laments, 'Clay tablets last four millennia but I can no longer access what I wrote on my Atari ST. . . .' Many readers will have no memory of what an Atari ST was.

The poem we call *Gilgamesh* is based on copies of a work assembled over a millennium after the earliest stories were written in Old Babylonian. Old Babylonian Bilgames morphed into Standard Babylonian Gilgamesh. A specific scribe, editor, collator, poet is given credit for bringing it all together. He may also have been an exorcist, magician, diviner, priest or seer; or a combination of these not unrelated vocations. He was active between 1300 and 1000 BCE. He may have been ancestor to a family of later scribes who retained his name. Though there is no agreement on what to call his vocation, he is certainly not what we would regard in the modern sense as an *author* or a *poet*. His contribution was curatorial. Though he may have added lines and passages, his main task was to forge a plausible whole out of scattered parts, a major feat but in creative terms a secondary one, working behind the scenes.

He goes by the name of Sin-leqi-unninni, which means 'The moon god Sin attends to my prayers'. The poet and editor John Clegg notes how 'the problems one faces as a reader, the lacunae and apparent irrelevancies and so on, were the same *sort* of problems as faced by the original compiler (even if they arose in different places and degrees).' Having organised the stories into a (more or less) continuous narrative of the heroes' adventures, Sin-leqi-unninni topped the poem with prefatory lines and tailed it with a reprise that echoes the opening but in a darker tone. Unusually for Standard Babylonian scribal work, Sin-leqi-unninni's name appears in a catalogue of texts and authors, not on any tablet of the poem itself.

No one can say for certain how much he contributed to the poem, but his name is, as Andrew George says, 'a convenient identifier for whatever intellect it was that produced the standardized text that was the vehicle for the Gilgamesh narrative in the first millennium.' The Standard Babylonian poem loses some of the directness and freshness of the Old Babylonian stories he was working from. His is not primarily what we would call a poetic imagination. Was he perhaps, as George suggests, 'a profound thinker, who gave the poem a structure and tone that were certainly the result of a deliberate and consistent policy to focus less on heroic grandeur and glory and more on human frailty and failure'? Or was he, as Stephen Greenblatt says, like Homer and the 'Genesis story teller', nothing less than 'a brilliant artist who was working with already existing materials, texts and oral legends that reached far, far back into the past'? Or was he less consistent and less decisive than either of these imagined figures, and his transformation of the given material less spectacular? How many of the arresting passages and metaphors are totally unattested in other and earlier versions?

In Middle Babylonian, judging from how many fragments survive over a wide area, there was a mess of versions or parts of versions (apprentice scribal exercises: far more beginnings survive than middles and ends). Sin-leqi-unninni appeared as in the Augean stables, Hercules's fifth labour, with his bucket, mop and shovel. He was not the only editor we know by name. Another organizer of even more disparate material, well before Sin-leqi-unninni, was Esagil-kin-apli, who, at the end of the second millennium, edited into canonical tablets some of the omen collections and other scattered material. His *Manual for Exorcists* was a substantial and essential medical text, identifying complaints and assigning them to the appropriate divine sender. Up to that point the omen traditions were in a tangle, which he voluminously sorted out.

Sin-leqi-unninni's *Gilgamesh* perhaps included twelve tablets. A tablet is neither a chapter nor a book: it is a count of lines— generally between 300 and 360, though some are shorter. Eleven of the tablets contain the narrative, with its brief introduction and its echoing coda, as though we had come full circle (which we haven't, quite). The twelfth tablet does not pertain directly to the poem in its shapely structure, but it tells about the Netherworld, how it is organised, and what happens when we go there.

Gilgamesh, the longest-standing poetic work in progress in history, is the most patient poem there will ever be. First it was entirely lost. Now it keeps being added to, corrected, adjusted. W. H. Auden quotes Paul Valéry as saying that a poem is never finished, it's finally abandoned. *Gilgamesh* will never be finished, but given the health of *Gilgamesh* scholarship, it is unlikely to be abandoned, either. Archaeologists and ruin-raiders turn up 'new' ancient tablets and fragments. The holes in the poem are about possibilities of recovery and meaning, spaces that await missing words and also invite the inventive engagement of scholar and lay reader.

The closest we can get will always be approximate. Even in the light cast by great scholarship, it can seem as though the journey has only just begun. Of the estimated 3600 lines of *Gilgamesh*, 3200 are known in whole or in part. Some of the parts are very small, and the complexity and ambiguity of the text will never let scholars rush ahead. In the next century or two the poem will not acquire even the relative stability of the Homeric texts. Assurbanipal did not require the standardization of the *Gilgamesh* text in the way that (it was once generally thought) the tyrant Peisistratos in sixth-century BCE Athens standardised the Homeric poems so that reciters at the Panathenaic Festivals would all sing, as it were, from the same hymn sheet. Even so, in the seventh and then in the fifth centuries BCE, complete versions of *Gilgamesh* existed, though differing from one another and differing also from their sources.

The British Museum has huge cuneiform holdings, and the task of translation began there. The emergence of *Gilgamesh* and the growth of Assyriology are down to a few remarkable modern advocates. First were the explorers who uncovered the great cities of Mesopotamia and thought to collect and send home not only the spectacular statuary but the mysterious, unreadable clay tablets they found. Unresting scholars follow them. With devotion and patient application, they deciphered the languages, finding human voices in the clay, and a king terrified of dying came back to the long half-life of poetry—of his particular poem.

· · ·

Among the first explorers to draw and then engrave the surviving inscriptions and tablets was Sir Austen Henry Layard, the

Victorian archaeologist who excavated at Nimrud and Nineveh (competing with the French, who got there first) and discovered some of the most famous Assyrian relief carvings and then momentously—in 1850—the remains at Nineveh (near modern Mosul in Iraq) of the great seventh-century BCE library of the last king of the neo-Assyrian empire, Assurbanipal. To Assurbanipal, a scholar—who claims to have undergone a thorough scribal education—and a severe ruler from 668 to 627 BCE, we owe a great deal. Perhaps also to his queen, Libbali-sarrat, who appears to have become learned, too. More of the standard twelve-tablet version of *Gilgamesh* was unearthed in 1853 by the Assyrian Christian Hormuzd Rassam, an assistant to Layard who accompanied him in his second, 1849–51 excursion to Iraq. Layard had by then changed vocation, having gone into politics and left the field to Rassam.

Assurbanipal's library contained texts he commissioned, confiscated or extorted from those he defeated or threatened. A few of these texts were books—as we must call the fine copies he collected: heavy, fragile, incised prototypes. These books included the most complete surviving text of *Gilgamesh,* among much else.

The flow of tablets and fragments has continued, from *bona fide* excavations and from other, darker sources. Ever since 1873 there has been a market for tablets, a white market and a black one that encourages archaeological piracy. Wars, with opportunistic raids on the great collections of the Middle East, have also disrupted the patterns of holding and scholarship. Assurbanipal's collection remains our widest (broken) window on the Mesopotamian literary past.

In 1851 Layard published the first volume of copies of the tablets, scrupulously made, the notation at the time undeciphered. Sir Henry Rawlinson, the so-called father of Assyriology, who began the task of deciphering cuneiform, supervised the publication of five great tomes of inscriptions between 1870 and 1884, copied faithfully by a number of well-trained hands. These were the crucial after-scribes whose work contributed to the recovery of the poem's millennia-dead languages.

For the layman first looking closely at a cuneiform tablet, the challenge of transcription, and then translation, looks impossible. It's not only the barbed look of the writing, how it seems to hang from rather than sit on its lines. There is also the fact that all the languages cuneiform was used to record are not only dead but, when the tablets were discovered, lost. Irving Finkel and Jonathan Taylor, in their handsome British Museum handbook entitled *Cuneiform* (2015), define the task.

The process of cuneiform decipherment was [. . .] multi-layered, for it demanded full grasp of how signs with multiple possible readings could function as writing, and the reconstruction of two unrelated and very dead languages [Old Babylonian and Standard Babylonian]. The achievement was, therefore, far greater than the decipherment of Egyptian hieroglyphic writing or Mycenaean Linear B.

As the different sounds that the same sign represented in Old Babylonian and Standard Babylonian were discovered, so transliteration changed, and meaning also. Standard Babylonian preserves Old Babylonian shapes and derives its authority from Old Babylonian, but it sounds and means differently, the structure of the language being as distinct from Old Babylonian as Latin is from Japanese. Old Babylonian may have been partly tonal, like Chinese, while Standard Babylonian is not believed to have been.

By 1880 both the Sumerian and Akkadian languages had been cracked, if not quite yet laid open. George Smith looms large in the history of Assyriology, the first salaried Assyriologist, employed by the British Museum in 1866, a man from a modest background, apprenticed as an engraver (at which he excelled), who made himself into a brilliant linguist, a pioneer throughout the 1860s and 1870s identifying among items in the British Museum's Kuyunjik collection numerous *Gilgamesh* fragments. These were largely from Assurbanipal's and other libraries of the period. A second source was the later libraries—fifth century—of Babylon, and of Uruk itself.

George Smith was the first modern man to read the Deluge Tablet. So excited was he when he read it that he ran about the room removing his clothes. He was the first to translate it into a modern language. Together with Gilgamesh, he and later scholars in all areas of Assyriology are the heroes of this book.

As the art of drawing tablets developed, it was an article of faith that viewers needed to see where words, lines and whole passages were missing. They also needed to be able to assess how much was missing within and between lines. This knowledge was a precondition to editing and interpretation. The size of a tablet, its edges and its thickness could also be important.

The German Assyriologist Arno Poebel, working with the collection of some 30,000 tablets and fragments at the University of Pennsylvania Museum of Archaeology and Anthropology in Philadelphia, produced some of the most perfect copies ever made. He also produced a still serviceable Old Babylonian grammar book. He became a Professor of Assyriology and Sumerology at the University of Chicago, but damaged his career and reputation and those of others because of an ingrained anti-Semitism.

In copying, Poebel would take as many as 1700 measurements with a ruler to get the spacings precisely correct—locating what was missing, where it was missing, how much was missing. The order of incisions mattered, how a scribe wedged and fanned his stylus's impressions, the depth of the cuts, and the texture of the tablet all contribute to the material meaning.

There is a significant topography of the clay surface, as there is a topography of any object with a surface, however regular, a topography best revealed in bright sunlight. It is tempting (though I am assured fanciful) to think that the act of reading might have included in some way the fact of texture, that the finger moved with the eye along the marks of the stylus, registering incisions whose depth and spacing might be expressive, indicating emphasis or—in terms of voice—volume, intonation. A scholar with mastery of Braille could tell us if the impressions can be read by finger-tip, in which case tablets might have been readable not only in a sunny courtyard, but at night. . . .

· · ·

No one institution possesses a full text of *Gilgamesh* in Standard Babylonian. It is now a jigsaw puzzle with pieces scattered across the Middle East, Europe, and the United States. The pieces of the jigsaw are mixed in with pieces of other puzzles, themselves spread across many centuries and several languages.

The feat of deciphering the dead languages that cuneiform recorded—Old Babylonian and Standard Babylonian first, but also Hittite, Elamite, Hurrian—was one of the toughest and least celebrated achievements of the Victorian age. Philologists' pay was poor, and they worked in difficult conditions, not in bright courtyards where the tablets were written but in under-illuminated archives and galleries of the British Museum and other institutions. There was no computer help. When George Smith read the Deluge, he did not have a team but broke the code himself. The world woke up at his news. Soon it was dozing once more, but with one eye alert for further surprises.

The tablets are not, for the most part, objects of aesthetic appeal, unlike the handsome stone-carved inscriptions that run across the surfaces of some sculptural panels and statuary. Today, when we are permitted to handle an ancient tablet, especially the apprentice copyists' tablets that fit in the palm, almost as if we were shaking hands with the original scribe, the sensation of living contact can be intense. The fine-grained river mud was rolled and patted into shape, sliced, lifted to the eye and, in dazzling sunlight of a scribal courtyard, under supervision, the cuneiform figures were incised. Racks were provided on which, once inscribed, the tablets were set to dry and harden.

Writing and reading cuneiform, which was first used as early as the mid-fourth millennium BCE, depends on a knowledge of the evolving symbols, of which there are up to a thousand, representing whole words, syllables, or portions such as initial letters. The symbols are not single in sense and sound. In different languages, and in those languages in different contexts, or at different periods, the same symbols can mean different things and be differently pronounced.

In their beginnings, the symbols were stripped-down images of things, pictures or logograms; these grew more stylised and easy to write the more they were used. At its simplest, the word 'mouth' is shown as a hole or space into which you can put a bread sign or a water sign to mean *eat* or *drink*. In time the sound, or part of the sound, of the thing or action originally named came to displace the name, as happens today with the evolving language of emojis, which can be phoneticised (an 'eye' for an 'I') and built into words. In time cuneiform evolved into a partly phonetic writing system, indebted but not connected to the writing conventions in which it took shape. Though the word signs remained in use to the very end and the logogrammatic tradition proved resilient, there was a progression from the largely figurative to the partly or wholly phonetic. The 'god' syllable *Anu*, for instance, the name of Ishtar's father and the father of the gods more generally, one of the deities who lives in his own temple in Uruk, survives as a logogram for the word *god* (*ilum*) and as a phonetic syllable *an*. It can also be prefixed to a name to identify a deity.

• • •

Half a century after the tablets were first discovered, *Gilgamesh* began to come into focus in English. That focus re-adjusts with each addition, and given the volatility of some of the content, it makes the news. This oldest poem of all becomes in the twentieth century a news resource, one that keeps altering with each discovery. The twenty-first century is no different, except the news travels faster.

And then, as I tirelessly reiterate, *Gilgamesh* is a poem without a poet. We have met Sin-leqi-unninni, the redactor. But we cannot speak of 'the Gilgamesh poet' in the way we speak of 'the Gawain poet'. There is no first text. There is no information, not even legend. Homer may be an invention, but there is a long tradition of the blind poet-bard and his poems; his life has been told, a fiction hovering henlike above her fictions. *Gilgamesh* cannot be provided with even a fictional author in this way. No first-person narrator sets things going with *Arma virumque cano* or ἄνδρα μοι ἔννεπε, μοῦσα. *Gilgamesh* comes filtered through different languages, not refined in them.

Given the poem's anonymity, its freedom from a specific sense of time and place, it is remarkable how rapidly poets, not only in English, responded to it. This very rootlessness may have been its attraction. It belongs nowhere; it belongs everywhere. Many responses to it were creative, attempting to incorporate and develop lessons learned from its material nature (fragmented, as though nature collaborated in the poem's surviving form) and from its themes, which are continuous with its material survival.

When we approach *Gilgamesh*, if we choose a translation that reflects the reality of the surviving texts in the ways that Andrew George's and Stephanie Dalley's British and (to a lesser extent) Benjamin Foster's American translations do, we are required to participate in the process of construing, trying to hear through the blanks: an anxious freedom for those of us accustomed to read fully authored and edited texts. Here scholarship is not allowed to run invisibly behind what we read: it spills into the foreground, it insists that we make decisions and choices. In order to do so, we read headnotes and footnotes, we consider surrounding scholarship, we equip and inform ourselves. We appreciate how suggestively alien, indeed how *original* in both senses, the poem is. And, necessarily, we are drawn into scholarship which is inseparable from the creative character of this most suggestive and at once most other, most alien, of poems. It forces scholars to take creative risks, and general readers to make scholarly choices.

WHAT SORT OF POEM? (1)

THE poem pretends to be spoken aloud. Is this a conceit, or was it a text for public recitation? If so, by whom? In the first tablet no narrator or story-teller is introduced. An audience attends, however, and the poem addresses that audience, posing rhetorical questions, anticipating responses, directing its attention.

Gilgamesh does not, at the outset, speak to us as individual readers but as members of an attentive group. We hear voices of men, women, monsters and gods. Some translators headline the speeches with speakers' names, suggesting dramatic form. Holding the book in their hands, individual readers imagine themselves as members of an audience. As readers we should remember to move our lips, we should hear what is being spoken.

Translators have fallen into the unreflecting habit of calling the poem an *epic* and then pushing their translations in directions familiar from epic poetry. *Gilgamesh* did not *know* it was 'the first epic poem'. It did not know it was an epic at all. Aristotle would have been uncomfortable with the appellation:

> As to that poetic imitation which is narrative in form and employs a single metre, the plot manifestly ought, as in a tragedy, to be constructed on dramatic principles. It should have for its subject a single action, whole and complete, with a beginning, a middle, and an end. It will thus resemble a living organism in all its unity, and produce the pleasure proper to it. It will differ in structure from historical compositions, which of necessity present not a single

action, but a single period, and all that happened within that period to one person or to many, little connected together as the events may be. It isn't straightforwardly *narrative* in form. It does not employ a single metre. It is not constructed on dramatic principles as is a tragedy. It does not concentrate on 'a single action, whole and complete, with a beginning, middle and end'. How organic is it—like a single living organism, or like a string of narrative organisms?*

If we approach it as epic, we put between it and ourselves the complex lenses of historical and theoretical expectations, rules and revisions of rules. When we approach any text with unauthorised generic anticipation, we limit our ability to identify what might actually be there. And we propose connections that are anachronistic and distorting. Even the ways in which we ask questions of a poem can anticipate, if not specific answers, then certain kinds of answer, certain kinds of limitation.

Even that scrupulous scholar Andrew George is occasionally drawn into anachronism. Writing in 2012, he declares, 'Modern readers easily identify with Gilgamesh as individual to individual, and recognize his existential struggle as their own, but magnified to an heroic scale.' I might, in George's sense, be tempted to 'identify with' Enkidu, or in a different spirit with Shamhat. *Gilgamesh* is at the level of narrative alien and remote, and to speak of the protagonist easily as an 'individual' in the sense we give the word today, and to set 'us' in apposition to him, is to draw the poem out of its wide orbit, historical and philosophical, into our narrow one. Such a strategy of 'identification', forcing Gilgamesh the king into an unjustified relevance, misleads

* *Poetics*, XXIII, "Epic Poetry."

us, blocking our access to a sense of the living original. George assumes modern readers share a community of natures (are we indeed *de facto* engaged in an existential struggle? and, if so, all of us in the same *kind* of struggle?). Between this homogenised 'us' and Gilgamesh, who is portrayed as a medieval Everyman or compared to a novel character from the nineteenth century, a bogus relationship is created. As soon as an exercise in assimilation begins, the poem blurs: we find ourselves gazing into something that might even be a mirror.

Great poetry is not always about ourselves in this way. If it were, a fragmented and treacherous text like *Gilgamesh* would have very little attraction for us. Instead, it is fascinating not only because of the linguistic challenges it poses but because it is *not* about an imagined 'ourselves'. It provides spaces—some of them fractured, some of them vertiginously remote—in which we are able to step out of our time and space and away from whatever our existential struggle might be, and to experience other possibilities.

Can we agree to approach the poem, if not on its own terms, which we cannot know with any certainty, then not on our terms, either? Can we strip from it some at least of the familiar patterns that poets, scholars and critics have applied down the short ages of its recovery? Can we avoid the term 'epic', with all that it specifically implies? It might make sense to break down Sin-leqi-unninni's great synthesised Standard Babylonian poem into its component Old Babylonian parts, the adventure and kingship stories, the traditional laments, the underworld journey. But the strategy of restoring to the poem some of its prehistory helps underline its generic non-conformity and variety and make it proof against anachronistic generic categories and critical approaches which themselves take over and dictate how we read, translate and interpret it.

If we come to distrust the 'epic' categorisation, other things follow. For example, we are assured that *Gilgamesh* emerged from an oral tradition. Stephen Greenblatt, in *The Rise and Fall of Adam and Eve,* insists that the Mesopotamian tablets (he does not distinguish between the Old Babylonian and the Standard Babylonian, though centuries separate them) 'almost certainly had behind them, as the wind in their sails, centuries of oral storytelling to which we can have no access'. Why 'almost certainly'? Why does the poem modulate into prose at two key points? Greenblatt also evokes the verse, beautifully but not persuasively, as 'these remarkable works of fragile breath'. The idea that the poem is the product of an oral tradition is widely shared, almost as an axiom. It fits comfortably with Homeric scholarship. But original oral tradition cannot be proven, and other explanations might make better poetic sense.

When literary historians affirm that the poem emerged from an oral tradition, are they referring to the Old Babylonian episodes or to the Standard Babylonian poem drawn from them, that Sin-leqi-unninni curated? The Standard Babylonian text lacks the mnemonic patterns that characterise the Homeric poems. There are verbatim repetitions of passages, to be sure, and there are some epithets, but the prosody is not regular in ways that would render the text memorable *in extenso* to a singer of tales. Because we believe that the poems out of which the so-called Homeric poems evolved were orally performed, and eventually written down and developed, it is tempting to project a similar pattern on the much earlier *Gilgamesh*, forgetting its complicated linguistic evolution. Earlier in time does not imply more primitive in culture, not least when we are comparing the sophisticated Standard Babylonian city-states with the emerging Homeric world. And George helpfully notes that not all long narrative poems from Babylonia that treat the deeds of the gods spring from an ancient oral tradition. The Creation Epic (*Enūma elish*) is an obvious case in point. This text, which tells of the rise of Marduk of Babylon to be king of the gods, and of his organization of the cosmos with his city in the middle, was clearly composed by a learned poet as a written composition.

A poem may be informed by narrative and oral traditions without having been, even originally, composed as or for performance.

Unlike in the *Odyssey* and the *Aeneid*, performance as such is not represented in *Gilgamesh*, unless we want to regard dialogue as suggesting dramatic presentation, with passages of repetition working as refrains. In that case we might as well describe the genre as dramatic, not epic.

• • •

Even in an originally oral tradition, when a poem is at last committed to clay, papyrus, parchment or paper, the volume, as it were, is turned off. We are left with running subtitles, hearing replaced by reading. Transcription changes the experience and therefore the nature of the poem. Gone is drum, lyre, or other musical accompaniment, if it had one, along with the voice or voices of recitation and performance, inflections denoting pace and response. Those who have hitherto been members of an audience, with a pooled interest and a shared response, now stand single, clutching the tablet. If we were dancing with a human form before, with voice and body and expression, we find ourselves now embracing an absence, less than a skeleton, and having ourselves to provide the warmth and motion, even the flesh.

We are no longer parts of an audience. Reading entails active generation.

It's also the case that, once the poem is written down, there is no longer any need to remember it. We can always look it up and read it, assuming we *can* read, when we return to it. Or we can ask the scribe, or a group of literate friends, to read it aloud. Once a text is on a clay tablet, it can be copied, improved, edited. We can add incidents, add scenes; and we can delete elements that are archaic or objectionable. Language evolves, and the first written version becomes obsolete; or antique and authoritative, stiffening into canonicity; or it inspires other works and causes the poem to evolve. The reader, the reviser, the revisitor, hears connections and perhaps emphasises them by changes to the text, by heightenings and deletions.

Dalley's account of the flowering of the scribal tradition is telling: 'Authorship of the oldest, traditional work,' she writes, was 'attributed to sages who were sent before the flood by the god Ea to bring civilisation to mankind'. After the flood, authors 'were honoured with sage-like status'. They were at their most active in the Kassite period (1650–1150 BCE), the late Bronze Age. This is when collecting and composing verses were at their height, a Golden rather than a Bronze Age in terms of poetry. Sin-leqi-unninni was active as a master scribe and lamentation priest. Another named scribe was Enheduana, the daughter of Sargon, king of Agade. She collected, edited, extended and handed on the Temple Hymns one thousand years before Sin-Leqi-Unninni.

WHAT SORT OF POEM? (2)

FOR the contemporary reader, N. K. Sandars's rendition is a good point of departure because it tells the story briskly, efficiently and smoothly. The reader gets a sense of narrative pace and is not troubled by those stylistic elements that slow down and complicate the philologically careful and textually alert readings that those gripped by the accelerated movement in Sandars should move on to next. Sandars enjoyed the story and communicates enjoyment in her style. But she ironed out the pleats, in particular the repetitions which take over for long stretches and are part of the poem's way of meaning. 'The assumptions you bring to the text', says Gabriel Josipovici, 'limit your capacity to see what is there.'

What might *Gilgamesh* have considered itself to be? Perhaps 'historical composition', chronicle, a form that has come up earlier in this account. George insists, 'The career of Gilgamesh, passed down by the king lists, omens and exorcistic texts as well as by narrative poetry, was to the Babylonians a historical reality. The ancients did not distinguish between Gilgamesh the hero, Gilgamesh the king and Gilgamesh the god.' The real and (to us) legendary King Gilgamesh are folded together. Was *Gilgamesh*, then, an instalment in the King narratives (there were poems about Gilgamesh's forebears, fragments of which survive)? Just how historical is the poem, and in what terms?

Gilgamesh built roads and dug wells (as when he and Enkidu went off to slay Humbaba). The Babylonian well-opening ritual includes a brief invocation of him. Wells were important not only because they brought water to the surface but because they connected ours with the Netherworld. Libations were poured to relieve the thirst of the departed spirits. In Gilgamesh's sun-bleached world, thirst and suffering are synonymous.

Gilgamesh dead, as nether-spirit for the Babylonians, seems to have become a benign force, acting as a Netherworld judge, though he survives in Islamic magic as Jiljamis, a spiteful demon. Humbaba, too, survives in this context.

If he actually lived, Gilgamesh ascended the throne of Uruk in the wake of some remarkable and, according to the Old Babylonian king lists, long-serving rulers. King Enmerkar is credited with the invention of writing on clay tablets. He is said to have incised a message in the earliest cuneiform, to convey an ultimatum to his enemy the Lord of Aratta. His messenger delivered the tablet to a puzzled ruler who couldn't read it. That message did not get through, then, and the Lord of Aratta was duly brought low in the conventional way.

But Enmerkar was not put off: he kept working on his new medium. He reigned for 420 years (or even, in one account, 900 years), so he had plenty of time to perfect it, pressing out the tablets from local mud, cutting the reed styluses, and using the shadows cast by the bright sunlight in his courtyards to evolve the signs.

The kings are foregrounded in the chronicles that survive in Standard Babylonian. Years are named after them. They make sure that the mighty works they commission are signed with their names. Shelley's Ozymandias is their truest heir.

And on the pedestal, these words appear:
My name is Ozymandias, King of Kings;
Look on my Works, ye Mighty, and despair!
Nothing beside remains. Round the decay

Of that colossal Wreck, boundless and bare
The lone and level sands stretch far away.

The written record is a key part of the ritual of remembering. If kings remember their forebears, they draw dignity from them but also (by example) stand a better chance of being remembered themselves. They restore the buildings of their ancestors in order to be seen themselves as pious, and to encourage their successors to pay the same attention to their legacies.

Some kings promoted themselves as learned, investing considerable effort in creating the record of their reign, to secure a place in memory, memory being one form of survival they could understand. For example, Shulgi of Ur (c. 2029–1982 BCE) claimed to be Gilgamesh's brother, regardless of their respective dates. He too was a son of the goddess Ninsun. He did not just hanker after divinity: he claimed actually to *be* a god even when he was alive. He said he had 'studied the scribal art from the tablets of Sumer and Akkad'; he mastered writing and numbers and accounting and languages (half a dozen), music and extispicy ('the liver is a mirror of heaven'). He was the first to mention *schools*.

Enmerkar is in a different league of kings from Shulgi, in legend and in history. He is said to have founded the city of Uruk itself, so he was actually (if he was actual) Gilgamesh's predecessor and perhaps his grandfather, real or adoptive. Enmerkar did not die of old age. He (or his father) vanished into the sea (which sea is not specified: Uruk was not on the coast). Perhaps he too was keen to avoid death and went off in search of Utanapishti. He did not come back. The modern historian David Rohl implausibly identifies Enmerkar with King Nimrod, familiar from the Bible as being responsible for erecting the ill-fated Tower of Babel. The passage in Genesis 10 (from the King James Version of the Bible) might seem to feed on some of the same material as *Gilgamesh*:

> And Cush begat Nimrod: he began to be a mighty one in the earth.
>
> He was a mighty hunter before the Lord [. . .]
>
> And the beginning of his kingdom was Babel, and Erech, and Accad, and Calneh, in the land of Shinar.
>
> Out of that land went forth Asshur, and builded Nineveh, and the city Rehoboth, and Calah,
>
> And Resen between Nineveh and Calah: the same is a great city.
>
> And the whole earth was of one language, and of one speech.
>
> And it came to pass, as they journeyed from the east, that they found a plain in the land of Shinar; and they dwelt there.
>
> And they said one to another, Go to, let us make brick, and burn them thoroughly. And they had brick for stone, and slime had they for mortar.
>
> And they said, Go to, let us build us a city and a tower, whose top may reach unto heaven; and let us make us a name, lest we be scattered abroad upon the face of the whole earth.
>
> And the Lord came down to see the city and the tower, which the children of men builded.
>
> And the Lord said, Behold, the people is one, and they have all one language; and this they begin to do: and now nothing will be restrained from them, which they have imagined to do.
>
> Go to, let us go down, and there confound their language, that they may not understand one another's speech.

So the Lord scattered them abroad from thence upon the
face of all the earth: and they left off to build the city.
  Therefore is the name of it called Babel; because the Lord
did there confound the language of all the earth. . . .

Legend and history collide, real dates and mythical ones re-
fuse to concur. Enmerkar (accounts vary) may have been suc-
ceeded by his general Lugalbanda, who reigned for 1200 years
and was eventually, though not immediately, succeeded by Gil-
gamesh, thought to have been his son. Gilgamesh's reign was
comparatively short, a mere 126 years. . . .

The King Lists were composed to establish the legitimacy and
lineage (deep-rooted in time) of the kings of Isin, portraying them
as successors in the great line of the kings of Ur. After Gilgamesh's
126 years, later kings' reigns were more modest, between thirty-
six and six years.

Gilgamesh has other roles to play in history, and in the leg-
ends that are continuous with it. We have already seen him as a
judge in the Netherworld, a divine or semi-divine function (al-
though it does not amount to the deathlessness to which he as-
pired and for which he went to the ends of the earth). In the
Netherworld he fulfills his chthonic duties and is sometimes
associated with Dumuzi, his own predecessor as king and
Ishtar's quondam husband, whom Gilgamesh, when he rejects
Ishtar, compares to a wounded bird; and Ningiszida, another
keeper of the Netherworld. Gilgamesh is also portrayed as a
ferryman, like Charon in classical myth, or his own ferryman
and companion in the return journey to Uruk, Ur-shanabi. As
though these were insufficient identities, his name was used in
Babylonian rituals of exorcism, and he was listed as a giant in
the non-Babylonian Book of Giants. One would expect the son of
the goddess Ninsun, 'Lady Wild Cow', to be a man of parts: he

is, after all, *almost* divine—but perhaps of not quite so many parts.

Is *Gilgamesh*, in Standard Babylonian terms, or the stories of Gilgamesh, in Old Babylonian terms, to be regarded as historical composition, then? Irving Finkel, in *The Ark before Noah: Decoding the Story of the Flood* (2014), says,

> Gilgamesh, we can be sure, was a real man. He was an early king of Uruk who founded a short-lived dynasty at the beginning of the historical period. All the surviving literary traditions about Gilgamesh point to a figure of power and charisma that long-outlasted his own lifetime. The cycle of stories that came to circulate about his name testify to this, and the impression that he was a man out of the same box as Alexander the Great, the impact of whose death led to narratives far beyond the sober scope of the historians who first tackled his life and times.

To the Standard Babylonians as to their Old Babylonian predecessors, hyperbole is part of recording events of the past: these things were accepted as real, even if not as 'literally' real as we expect history to be. (In those days there were giants in the earth.) Certainly the interfering gods had to be dealt with on a daily basis, housed in handsome temples, nourished and appeased; and the rivers that sustained life also flooded and destroyed it. The Netherworld was a continual concern. And the Ends of the World, which Gilgamesh visits? The world has ends: the ancient cosmos was bounded by water, the world not yet round and barrelling through space as part of a solar system.

Or might *Gilgamesh* have regarded itself as a religious poem? Can one distinguish secular from religious in a world so shot through with divinities with contradictory divine intentions, in which men's survival depends on how they play the gods off against one another, given their overgrown human passions, resentments and pettinesses?

Gilgamesh participates, one way and another, in almost all the forms of Old Babylonian and Standard Babylonian literature that survive. It is a narrative composition with historical and mythological dimensions. It includes praise poetry, prayers, debate, dialogue, diatribe, and of course lament, in which the later tablets abound. It has all the elements of wisdom literature. And it is laced with proverbial phrases. Perhaps that is as close as we can get to assigning it to a genre: to say that it is an anthology of genres. Andrew George, in arguing in favour of genre and genre theory and what it can teach us about the poem, concedes,

> Sumerian [Old Babylonian] and Akkadian [Standard Babylonian] are poor in generic terminology, and many have noted the lack of a native poetics [. . .]. In Sumerian, generic terminology developed to distinguish between compositions that were performed in different manners or to different musical accompaniment [. . .]. Akkadian possesses words that surely make generic distinctions also but, again, these labels are mostly performative and not literary [. . .]. The written culture of the Babylonians is not given to analysis or prescription of the kind developed by classical writers.

He also finds ten distinct Akkadian literary categories represented in *Gilgamesh*.

Getting away from classical and subsequent generic terms, we can say (uncontroversially, I hope) that *Gilgamesh* is an *agon* in a number of (non-generic) senses: a wrestling contest, a wider combat, a religious conflict, a profound confrontation with the *almost* unbendable facts of human fate. It is the story of the growth and struggle of a central figure. It could be seen as a double *agon*, with Enkidu's momentous change and death as a necessary sub-plot. But his death comes too early for him to be given equal billing with the king.

Does an *agon* require that we 'identify with' the principal figure? Neither Enkidu nor Gilgamesh is representative, neither is an everyman, neither is *character* enough for us to read ourselves into him. There is nothing conventional about them: a wild man formed out of river clay, then 'civilized'; a king, part god but stuck in time, part man but unable to control his fate. How do we relate to the plots? It is an important question because, if we come to love the poem, as it is hard not to do after a careful and sustained acquaintance with it, the sense of that love is quite different from what we feel for more familiar, generically determinate works. It does and gives something exceptional to readers, something that follows not only from the remote figures and their world, but from our experience of *making*, investing our own critical and creative energies, in the process of reading. We play a primary role in the poem, we occupy it as we might a great sculpture: a broken form we—in reading—mend, a space we fill out, in which we find things we did not know, that change us.

The poem not being an epic, what title should we give it? Should we go by its incipit (like calling the *Aeneid* by its opening phrase, *Arma virumque* or *Arms and the Man,* in the manner of George Bernard Shaw)? Do we prefer *The Adventures of Gilgamesh*? *The Tale of Gilgamesh*? Or, to honour the poem's favourite figure, *Gilgamesh and Enkidu*? The best title is plain *Gilgamesh*. Even in its damaged state, the poem can make its way without the aid of a subtitle or auxiliary, on its own two feet.

And how big are those feet? A triple cubit.

GILGAMESH READS US

ASK a poem, especially a poem remote in time and culture, how it sees us. Who does it think *we* are? The answer comes in several kinds of critical and creative engagement which in one form or another *Gilgamesh* occasions.

My contemporaries among the poets, and not only those who have translated and adapted it, might have answers to give *Gilgamesh*. The poem meant something to me when I was in my early twenties; I assumed it had touched and maybe stayed with others. Their responses informed this book and illuminated my re-reading, making it an experience shared in the way the poem itself proposes.

I also joined for a few weeks in Cambridge a University of the Third Age reading group run by Professor Nicolas Postgate in which the students inched their way through *Gilgamesh* in the Standard Babylonian, doing up to a dozen lines an hour. The passages of verbatim repetition, which some translators gloss over and some readers find tedious and skip, the group welcomed with a sense of acceleration. Repetitions function as readerly mnemonics, drawing lines of connection within the poem and establishing the authority of the narrative. If an event is predicted in a dream, and then occurs in the very same language as that used in the prediction, it tells us how events inhere in time. Free will has little space in such a world. Given the nature of omens and dreams, dramatic suspense is unknown: the pleasure is to see how what is anticipated comes about, expanding the terms in which it was predicted. What reassures us as good Standard

Babylonians (but does not excite us as modern readers) is that the foreknown order holds. Narrative time has been transformed into a stable, almost a spatial structure in the narrative.

As general readers, we arrive at the translated poem expecting to read as we might the more complete texts of Homer or Virgil, to ride the text, following patterned language into a story where surprises, accidents and reversals occur. *Gilgamesh* resists expectations of this kind, too. We learn a different way of reading. Or we resort to one of the translations that familiarise the poem, cure it of its vexing difference and make it speak a language ('plain American which cats and dogs can read', as Marianne Moore says) that people are more likely to buy.

Gilgamesh can be made relevant to contemporary civic and political issues, as in Edwin Morgan's 2005 dramatic adaptation. It keeps thematic faith with the original, but this entails breaking faith with the original's form and style. It is the form of the original, and the things that the form keeps dry, the rhetorics it avoids, the objects and scenes it chooses *not* to describe, that are at the heart of its suggestive poetic economy. Morgan uses a variety of dialects and social registers, including Glasgow Scots. He adds players, and his play speaks in what novelist Ali Smith calls 'bantering rhyming couplets, which make it blunt and lyrical at the same time'. He enhances the dialogue the poem provides, but he turns it decisively to his own political ends. Ali Smith notes, 'Selflessness and open-armed anonymity are at the centre of all [Morgan's] art'. 'Open-armed anonymity' well describes the formal resource that *Gilgamesh* most usefully makes available.

Paul Muldoon says of Robert Frost that he 'was important to me early on because his line, his tone of voice, was so much a bare canvas'. A bare canvas: it is the hardest space for a poet to clear for the reader. Frost does it, Whitman does it, and *Gilgamesh*, so that what flows from it is an empowering energy that charges each reader differently, according to her or his abilities and needs.

Benjamin Foster's faithful 2001 translation may have inspired Morgan. Foster makes a feature of dialogue, as though the poem might indeed originally have been performed as a dramatic or a seasonal ritual.

Scholarly translations keep the uncomfortable, always instructive difference of the original in constant view. They aren't threatened by modern versions in English prose and verse, and hold their own against the picture book, comic book, manga and stage versions, and those composed for the concert hall. My favourite *Gilgamesh* surprise was in *Star Trek: The Next Generation*, when Picard, Patrick Stewart's character, movingly recites an abbreviated version of the Bull of Heaven passage to the dying Tamarian captain Dathon, whose language Picard is acquiring, to bring about a cessation of hostilities.*

•   •   •

In an ideal world, what English form would best suit *Gilgamesh*? All poet-translators approach with their own specific tool kit, and the translation they make reveals the contents of their mind and culture quite as much as it tells us about the original poem. A text is a cultural product with specific cultural referents. Remove the supporting culture and those referents fade. With *Gilgamesh*, even the language, that most complex set of referents in structure, rhythms and patterns, its etymologies and other connections, loses force: no poet-translator (and few of those who write about it, myself included) has mastered it. We lack the centuries of critical and philological response that inform (and to some extent determine) our reading of other classics. *Gilgamesh*'s

* https://www.youtube.com/watch?v=WCmwClf0F8g.

creative presence in our literatures begins in the twentieth century. The poem comes to be read with an appropriative, anachronising, modern eye.

Homer exists in different translations for different generations. He is translated into the dominant styles of an age, grows old with the literature that surrounds him (as Chapman grows old with Jonson and Shakespeare) and is then re-translated, rejuvenated, in the style of the next. This happens most eloquently in the ages in which there are dominant styles and decorums and the translator either works with or against them.

Given the construction of the verse, or rather, the double-construction, the half-lines paralleling stress patterns and being by and large organised into two-line units, what English form would best accommodate it? One can imagine a translation into couplets that honoured the original disposition, tetrameter couplets, or couplets in the manner of Dryden, not the disjunctive couplets of Pope. Perhaps more appropriately, one might imagine a translation into a modified Persian *ghazal* form, paired lines with a prosodic echo, tactful assonance and predictive repetition rather than rhyme. The *ghazal* has its roots in the extended neighbourhood of *Gilgamesh*. A poet with the technical means and cultural radicalism of the (late) Australian Judith Wright, or the Anglo-Persian Mimi Khalvati, or the American Marilyn Hacker, would have the tact to do the poem justice; and their own thematic concerns include many of those in the ancient poem. All the modern poets who suggest themselves to me as potential translators happen to be female.

Our diverse age, or ailing cultural diaspora, lacks literary and cultural coherence. It also lacks respect for the authority not only of critics but of informed scholars. The classics have long been vulnerable to modernist and post-modern raiding parties. Gilgamesh, a new arrival, without the ramparts of historical and critical writing that surround Homer and Virgil and Dante, is welcomed by a bewildering array of enthusiasts, each feeling entitled to a piece—a shard—of the action. It is as though not one damaged poem has arrived, but many, different in character and inflection, though equally fragmented and following a similar narrative route-map.

Philip Terry's unusual translation into 'Globish' effects a powerful 'restrangement' of a poem that Sandars domesticated in prose and Stephen Mitchell tricked out in verse. By means of a coherent experiment, Terry focuses our attention on the remote original, the languages in which it was conceived and set down. Terry's is an inventive and resonant version, its dialect a severe and a liberating constraint.* His incipit is worth attending to here for its ingenuity, its emphasis on the syllabic prosody in counterpoint to the syntax, the bizarre diction. I am unhappy with his introduction of a first-person narrator, and his use of a future tense soon succumbs to the stiffened present. He argues that much of the poem is, or will be, in Gilgamesh's voice, and his narrator's voice at times seems to fold into the voice of the king. And yet with the baton of his two-syllable marker, which is intolerant of words and breaks them like rhythmic kindling, he conducts our reading pace and tone of voice:

I will | sing of | the one | who see | the bot | tom . . .
of he | who know | all I | will tell | the . . . | story

---

* 'Translating, or versioning, *Gilgamesh* using the 1500-word vocabulary of Globish (from the words "global" and "English") put together by Jean-Paul Nerrière for business purposes, which he considered the world dialect of the third millennium, may look like a peculiar and arbitrary thing to do. There are some powerful and logical reasons underpinning this experiment in translation.' Philip Terry, contributing to the conference '"The Bearer-Beings": Portable Stories in Dislocated Times', convened by Professor Marina Warner at St Anne's College, Oxford, May 2016.

+++in | ~~the old~~ | way . . . | from be | ginning | to end
+++the | wise ~~one~~ | he who | know ev | ery | thing DIC |
   TATOR
who see | the sec | ret thing | that no | man see | before
open | the sec | ret place | that no | man op | en be |
   fore . . .
and bring | back word | of the | time be | fore the | great
   wave.

Prosody is given precedence over syntax: we are not allowed to separate sound and sense. We can't read ahead, much less scan, raiding the lines for stable sense. We have to *read* them; indeed, to make our way through the poem we soon start to read aloud. Terry deals with the gaps and erasures in a consistent way that adds to the poem's staccato fluency and does not let us forget we are in alien territory.

HOW YOU TELL IT

AS an index of the evolving fashions in translation, we can trace one scene through a handful of modern versions, to see how poets and scholars deal with the poem's language and one of its awkward themes, that of Enkidu's sexual relations with Shamhat and his 'civilisation' at her hands. The euphemisms of the earlier translations give way to more graphic, anachronistic and sensationalising approaches. Attention moves down from 'bosom' as a metonym to crotch, and the sense of sight is soon enhanced with touch and smell. Discretion gives way to prurience.

First is R. Campbell Thompson's relatively chaste 1928 scholarly version in *The Epic of Gilgamesh: Text, Transliteration and Notes*. He has risked English hexameters, believing that the poem should be rendered into a consistent poetic form, and since he calls his version an epic, he chooses the standard measure used in Greek and Latin epics.

> The girl, displaying her bosom,
> Shew'd him her comeliness, (yea) so that he of her beauty
> possess'd him,
> Bashful she was not, (but) ravish'd the soul of him,
> loosing her mantle,
> So that he clasp'd her, (and then) with the wiles of a
> woman she plied him,
> Holding her unto his breast.
> ('Twas thus that) Enkidu dallied

Six days, (aye) seven nights, with the courtesan-girl in his
mating.
Sated at length with her charms, he turn'd his face to his
cattle,
O the gazelles, (how) they scamper'd away, as soon as
they saw him!
Him, yea, Enkidu,—fled from his presence the beasts of
the desert!

The interjections and archaisms make it comical in its careful
propriety. Shamhat is a seductress and Enkidu is a conventional
male who, having had enough, turns back to his quondam com-
panions, the animals. Thompson is content with stereotypes—of
his own rather than of *Gilgamesh's* culture. Other early transla-
tions follow the same pattern of suggestive obliquity. They do
not linger.

Almost three decades later, how varnished and prim E. A.
Speiser's 1955 version, reprinted in *Ancient Near Eastern Texts Re-
lating to the New Testament*, seems. Speiser is a major scholar but
not a natural poet. He has an instinct for cliché. The lack of any
formal engagement leaves his free verse without a pattern, oc-
casionally striving for sound effects but without an integrating
imagination or prosody.

The lass beheld him, the savage-man,
The barbarous fellow from the depths of the steppe:
'There he is, O lass! Free thy breasts,
Bare thy bosom that he may possess thy ripeness!
Be not bashful! Welcome his ardor!
As soon as he sees thee, he will draw near to thee.
Lay aside thy cloth that he may rest upon thee.

Treat him, the savage, to a woman's task!
Reject him will his wild beasts that grew up on his steppe,
As his love is drawn unto thee.'
The lass freed her breasts, bared her bosom,
And he possessed her ripeness.
She was not bashful as she welcomed his ardor.
She laid aside her cloth and he rested upon her.
She treated him, the savage, to a woman's task,
As his love was drawn unto her.
After six days and seven nights Enkidu comes forth,
He set his face toward his wild beasts.

The would-be free verse is ghosted by the iambic. The translation cries out for form.

We are already familiar with N. K. Sandars's 1960 *The Epic of Gilgamesh*. Her Shamhat is given more agency ('she made herself naked and welcomed his eagerness'): the poem understands her gendered perspective. This is Enkidu's first lesson in sex, and she is an experienced and feisty instructor.

> She was not ashamed to take him, she made herself naked and welcomed his eagerness; as he lay on her murmuring love she taught him the woman's art. For six days and seven nights they lay together, for Enkidu had forgotten his home in the hills; but when he was satisfied he went back to the wild beasts. Then, when the gazelle saw him, they bolted away; when the wild creatures saw him, they fled.

It all happens much too fast. No body parts are mentioned: the version keeps faith in this sense with the original. We hear murmuring, but we see and smell nothing. Even so, there is an understated erotic charge to which it is hard not to respond, a charge due to the realisation, if that is the right expression, of the female perspective.

Ten years later, in 1970, Nigel Dennis takes this scene and makes a separate narrative of it in his collection *Poems of the Mediterranean and Middle East*. He is fascinated by Shamhat as a woman, and by sex as a phenomenon. He lingers.

[She] bares her breasts and drops her skirt;
And the lion and panther go their way,
And the deer trot by to drink their fill.
But Enkidu starts, and snuffs the air,
The air of Ishtar, the temple whore;
And his hands go out, his fingers search:
And she takes his hands and presses close
And guides him into the seat of love
While the animals drink at the water hole.
[. . .]
For six days and for seven nights
Enkidu harries the seat of love;
For six days and for seven nights
The savage learns, the whore instructs;
Enjoying his eagerness,
Destroying his innocence,
Teaching him secrets
Unknown to beasts;
Until on the seventh morning,
Like a sower that has emptied his sack
And is tired of his long seeding
And longs for the water-pitcher and the reed-bed,
Enkidu withdraws from Ishtar's field
And takes the path to the water-hole.

But Ishtar's sweat runs down his skin
And human tricks run through his head;
The lion roars, the panther screams;
The nosing deer pick up the stench:
And when Enkidu bends to drink
Then every brute runs for his life;
Runs to the hills to lose his stink . . .

He cannot resist excessive imagery and off-the-peg Freudian metaphor. The nose comes into play. The original becomes a pretext for something else. Formally, the line units are sound, and free verse comes into its own, but there is little tension in the lines.

How much more powerful is the condensation of the episode into two lines in Louis Zukofsky's epic *"A"*, Canto 23 (completed in 1974), in which Enkidu is re-named One Kid, one of Zukofsky's characteristic approaches to replicating the form-sound of the original he was working from.

Strongest sent, his harlot went,
One Kid exulted until unmanned.

The whole of *"A"* is composed in five-word lines, a suggestive extension of syllabics. *Gilgamesh* is a marker for Zukofsky, as for Olson, though in Zukofsky's case the challenges the poem offers are less immediately thematic than formal.

Maureen Gallery Kovacs's *The Epic of Gilgamesh*, published in 1989, looks as though it is in verse, but despite the lineation the movement is entirely that of prose, with long arhythmic lines interspersed with shorter runs that veer towards metre without quite getting there.

Shamhat unclutched her bosom, exposed her sex, and he
   took in her voluptuousness.
She was not restrained, but took his energy.
She spread out her robe and he lay upon her,
she performed for the primitive the task of womankind.
   His lust groaned over her;
for six days and seven nights Enkidu stayed aroused, and
   had intercourse with the harlot
until he was sated with her charms.
But when he turned his attention to his animals,
the gazelles saw Enkidu and darted off,
the wild animals distanced themselves from his body.

There is no titillation in the language, and as with Sandars the
perspective is Shamhat's: 'His lust groaned over her' and (she
takes no pleasure from her vocation) he has intercourse with her,
rather a clinical account of the open-air proceedings.

Stephanie Dalley, by contrast, in *Myths from Mesopotamia*
(1989), is forthright. Shamhat calls the shots, and there is a sense
(not overplayed) of smell and of the corruption of Enkidu's once
natural self. Sex has changed him into something else, we are
not yet quite sure what:

Shamhat loosened her undergarments, opened her legs
   and he took in her attractions
She did not pull away. She took wind of him,
Spread open her garments, and he lay upon her.
She did for him, the primitive man, as women do.
His love-making he lavished upon her.
For six days and seven nights Enkidu was aroused and
   poured himself into Shamhat.
When he was sated with her charms,

He set his face towards the open country of his cattle.
The gazelles saw Enkidu and scattered,
The cattle of open country kept away from his body.

Again, with Dalley the verse line is not under formal pressure. It is plain narrative, and the incident is not memorable as language. Jenny Lewis (2018), by contrast, brings Shamhat to the foreground, where she and Enkidu are given equal definition in balanced quatrains. This is not intercourse but love-making.

Shamhat was sitting | quiet by the pool's edge
Watching the flickering | fish in the shallows
When all of a sudden | he stood before her
The wild man was suddenly | standing before her.

The *hierodule* gasped | as he bent to touch her
Stroking her hair | like the fur of an animal
Stroking her thighs | like the flanks of an animal
As he caressed her | he sang to her softly.

Inanna looked down | blessing the lovers
Six nights, seven days | their bodies were joined
Six nights, seven days | their flesh was one flesh
Six nights, seven days | their spirits were one.

On day number seven | they rested together
Then Enkidu set off | to re-join his herd
But now gazelles ran | flung fearful glances
Hoof-beats soon distant | a patter of thunder.

It is fanciful, material is added—Shamhat's physical response to Enkidu's touch, the physiological particularity, Inanna's blessing of the lovers, the language from the marriage service—so that when Enkidu tries to return to the herd, the herd's response, which in the other translations seems natural and justified, here seems wilful. The sacramental should not play out in quite this way. The formal constraints the poet has given herself add to rather than refine the content.

The most inventive and wayward of the translations is also truest to the spirit of the original. In *Dictator* Philip Terry, working within the constraints of the diction of 'Globish', with his insistent cross-hatching bar marks which make us invest equally in each syllable pair, the prosodic intention over-riding the word unit, drills down unsentimentally into the sexual scene. There is no moral ambiguity about what is happening to Enkidu (WILD-MAN) in this transformation. We must remember that the poet is constrained by his chosen diction and has to invent ways of saying what the host language is not designed to say.

> The mag | azine | girl see | he the | man be | fore cul |
>   ture +++
> the wild | action | man from | the far | mountain
> "Here be | the man | party | girl get | ready | for a | kiss
>   +++
> Open | you leg | show WILD | MAN you | love box
> Hold no | thing back | make he | breathe hard
> When he | see you | he mouth | will op | en . . .
> Then he | will come | close to | take a | look +++
> Take off | you skirt | so he | can . . . | screw you
> Make this | man be | fore cul | ture know | what a | girl
>   can | do . . .
> The an | imal | who grow | up in | the wild | will run |
>   away | and de | sert he
> He will | push he | body | in to | you love | box . . ."

The mag | azine | girl ~~take~~ | ~~off~~ she | pants and | open |
   she leg | and he | strike+++ | like a | thunder | storm
, +++
She do | not hold | back she | make he | ~~breathe hard~~
She spread | out she | skirt . . . | so he | can lie | ~~on top~~
She make | the man | before | culture | know what | a wo |
   man | can do
He have | ++++++ | a hard | on+++
He have | ++++++ | a sec | ond hard | on+++
++++++ | ++++++ | a third | ++++++ | ++++++
He come | all ov | er she | face+++
++++++ | all ov | er she | +++ hair
++++++ | all ov | er she | breast+++
Six day | and se | ven night | WILDMAN | ~~screw the~~ |
   ~~sex girl~~

When WILD | MAN have | enough | of the | top shelf |
   girl . . .
he turn | to look | for the | . . . an | imal | ++++++
When they | see WILD | MAN the | wild horse | run in | a
   great | wheel . . .
When they | see WILD | MAN the | big cat | run in | to
   the | forest
And the | wild pig | dig in | the dirt
All . . . | the an | imal | of the | wild run | away | and des |
   ert he

Where possible, the gaps correspond to breaks in the text. The
translator has allowed himself to exceed the original, but within
that license he deploys exclusively the formal conventions of
Standard Babylonian verse, in particular the verbatim repetitions

that, whatever effects they have elsewhere, spice up the generic sex with coarse humour. The scene is moving; it is also funny. And at the end it is deeply sad, in ways it could not have been had it observed a more chaste restraint: human acts of kind have consequences that Enkidu in no way anticipated. The sad fact is that he had no will and no choice in the matter: it was only after the experience with Shamhat that he became self-conscious.

Postface

'GILGAMESH is a confusion of stories. There is, first, the broken story of the poem itself. Then, the story of why the clay tablets it was written on got broken into so many fragments, scattered over a vast area from Turkey to southern Iran, and was lost for millennia.'

This is how Sin-leqi-unninni would have introduced his conclusion, had he been the author of this book rather than a more fundamental redactor. Give the argument the impression of a shape, he would have said to himself. The return to the beginning, the uroboros. He might also have listed the many musical and opera 'versions' that have made the confusion of stories and approaches more or less melodic, including the Czech composer Bohuslav Martinů's 1955 *Epic of Gilgamesh*: choral work, five or more operatic versions, two in Turkish, one each in Danish, Serbian and Italian. He might have listed the novels drawn from or on the poem, including Philip Roth's *The Great American Novel* (1973), where we encounter the extraordinary baseball pitcher Gil Gamesh; and one version attributed to Saddam Hussein; the film and television debts, the comic books and mangas, the board games, artists' books and works of art—including the memorable paintings of Anselm Kiefer. Theodore Ziolkowski's book *Gilgamesh among Us: Modern Encounters with the Ancient Epic* (2011) is a study of the *brand* Gilgamesh has become.

The poem, despite its huge success as a cultural phenomenon in Europe and elsewhere, still awaits readers willing to step away from received dogma that tells us to read it as an early manifestation of the European epic, to consider it as rooted in an oral tradition, to provide it with a coherent narrator and the kinds of audience Homer and Virgil seem to have prepared for us. The formal and thematic questions the poem would like to raise are fascinating, and were it possible for us to read them without bias and answer them from the text as we currently have it, we would do the poem justice and bring its actual resources into play in our reading, criticism and poetic practice.

The English versions that lead us to the threshold of the poem are those prepared by the scholars, Andrew George in particular. His engagement makes limited concessions to what the age demands. It has no illusion that he might be composing poetry in his own right. His porous versions are readable in part because they remain focused on what we have of the original and do not pretend to take independent flight. Their secondary nature highlights the primary texts that hover just beyond their reach, and ours. But they bring them tantalisingly close.

Scholarly integrity prevents such translators from grouting over the cracks and filling in the larger gaps with anything more than carefully supported conjecture. Andrew George writes, 'Assyriology is traditionally a historicist discipline, founded on the evidence of known facts.' These are not Gradgrindian facts. His is an ambitious but realistic attempt to understand the languages in which the poem was composed and preserved and the alien cultures that produced them. With him and his kin, we should learn to acknowledge and embrace an otherness which is an as yet under-exploited resource for us as readers and writers and even, if we can get our heads around the phenomenon of the authorless poem, as theorists.

Bibliography

EDITIONS, TRANSLATIONS, ADAPTATIONS

Dalley, Stephanie. *Myths from Mesopotamia: Creation, the Flood, Gilgamesh, and Others*. New York: Oxford University Press, 1989.

Davis, Gerald J., trans. *Gilgamesh: The New Translation*. Bridgeport, CT: Insignia Publishing, 2014.

Ferry, David, trans. *Gilgamesh: A New Rendering in English Verse*. New York: Farrar, Straus and Giroux, 1992.

Foster, Benjamin R., ed. *The Epic of Gilgamesh: A Norton Critical Edition*. New York: W. W. Norton, 2001.

Gardner, John, and John Maier, eds. *Gilgamesh*. New York: Vintage Books, 1985.

George, Andrew, trans and ed. *The Babylonian Gilgamesh Epic: Critical Edition and Cuneiform Texts*. London: Oxford University Press, 2003.

George, Andrew, trans. and ed. *The Epic of Gilgamesh: The Babylonian Epic Poem and Other Texts in Akkadian and Sumerian*. New York: Penguin Classics, 1999.

Griffiths, Bill. *The Story of the Flood from Gilgamesh*. London: Pirate Press and Consortium of London Presses, [1975].

Jastro, Morris, and Albert T. Clay, ed. and trans. *The Epic of Gilgamesh: An Old Babylonian Version*. New Haven, CT: Yale University Press, 1920; San Diego: The Book Tree, 2003.

Komunyakaa, Yusef, and Chad Gracia, dramatisation. *Gilgamesh: A Verse Play*. Middletown, CT: Wesleyan University Press, 2009.

Kovacs, Maureen Gallery, trans. and ed. *The Epic of Gilgamesh*. Stanford, CA: Stanford University Press, 1989.

Lewis, Jenny. *Gilgamesh Retold*. Manchester: Carcanet, 2018.

Mason, Herbert. *Gilgamesh: A Verse Narrative*. New York: Penguin Books, 1970.

Mitchell, Stephen, trans. and ed. *Gilgamesh: A New English Version*. London: Profile Books, 2004.

Morgan, Edwin, dramatisation. *The Play of Gilgamesh*. Manchester: Carcanet, 2005.

Sandars, N. K., trans. and ed. *The Epic of Gilgamesh*. London: Penguin Classics, 1972 [1960].

Speiser, E. A. *Ancient Near Eastern Texts Relating to the New Testament.* Princeton, NJ: Princeton University Press, 1955.

Stephany, Timothy J., trans. *The Gilgamesh Cycle: A 5,000 Year Old Epic Poem with Zodiacal Connections*. N.p., 2013, 2014.

Temple, Robert, trans. *He Who Saw Everything: A Verse Translation of the Epic of Gilgamesh*. London: Rider, Random Century, 1991.

Terry, Philip. *Dictator*. Manchester: Carcanet, 2018.

Thompson, R. Campbell. *The Epic of Gilgamesh: Text, Transliteration and Notes*. Oxford: Clarendon Press, 1928.

Wall, Alan. *Gilgamesh*. Bristol: Shearsman Books, 2008.

CONTEXT, COMMENTARY, CRITICISM

Black, Jeremy, and Anthony Green. *Gods, Demons and Symbols of Ancient Mesopotamia: An Illustrated Dictionary*. Austin: University of Texas Press, 1992.

Burkert, Walter. *Babylon, Memphis, Persepolis: Eastern Contexts of Greek Culture*. Cambridge, MA: Harvard University Press, 2004.

Damrosch, David. *The Buried Book: The Loss and Rediscovery of the Great Epic of Gilgamesh*. New York: Henry Holt, 2006.

Finkel, Irving. *The Ark before Noah: Decoding the Story of the Flood*. London: Hodder and Stoughton, 2014.

Finkel, Irving, and Jonathan Taylor. *Cuneiform*. London: The British Museum, 2015.

Greenblatt, Stephen. *The Rise and Fall of Adam and Eve*. London: Bodley Head, 2017.

Heidel, Alexander. *The Gilgamesh Epic and Old Testament Parallels*. Chicago: University of Chicago Press, 1972.

Jacobsen, Thorkild. *The Treasures of Darkness: A History of Mesopotamian Religion*. New Haven, CT: Yale University Press, 1976. (Most of the essays originally published in *The Intellectual Adventure of Ancient Man*, ed. H. Frankfort et al., Chicago, 1946.)

Lord, Albert B. *The Singer of Tales*. Cambridge, MA: Harvard University Press, 1946, 1963.

Maier, John. *Gilgamesh: A Reader*. Wauconda, IL: Bolchazy-Carducci, 2001.

Olson, Charles. *Collected Poems*. Oakland: University of California Press, 1997.

Olson, Charles. *Collected Prose*. Oakland: University of California Press, 1997.

Poebel, Arno. *Studies in Akkadian Grammar*. Chicago: University of Chicago Press, 1939.

Sayce, Archibald Henry. *An Elementary Grammar with Full Syllabary and Progressive Reading Book, of the Assyrian Language, in the Cuneiform Type*. Cambridge: Cambridge University Press, 2014 [1875].

Tigay, Jeffrey H. *The Evolution of the Gilgamesh Epic*. Philadelphia: University of Pennsylvania Press, 1982.

Walls, N. *Desire, Discord, and Death: Approaches to Ancient Near Eastern Myth*. Boston: American Schools of Oriental Research, 2001.

Ziolkowski, Theodore. *Gilgamesh among Us: Modern Encounters with the Ancient Epic*. Ithaca, NY: Cornell University Press, 2011.

ALSO

Batchelor, Paul. 'An Outsider Still: An Interview with Bill Griffiths', http://www.paulbatchelor.co.uk/billgriffithsinterview.html.

Brady, Andrea. *Wildfire: A Verse Essay on Obscurity and Illumination*. San Francisco: Krupskaya, 2010.

Dennis, Nigel. *Exotics: Poems of the Mediterranean and Middle East*. New York: Vanguard Press, 1970.

Fenton, James. 'Signs of the Times', reviewing Stephen Mitchell's *Gilgamesh*. *Guardian*, 6 November 2004.

George, Andrew. 'The Mayfly on the River: Individual and Collective Destiny in the Epic of Gilgamesh'. *Kaskal* 9 (2012).

Housman, A. E. 'The Application of Thought to Textual Criticism'. In *Collected Poems and Selected Prose*. Harmondsworth: Penguin Books, 1988.

Huchel, Peter. *The Garden of Theophrastus: Selected Poems*. Manchester: Carcanet Press, 1983.

Langley, R. F. 'Tin Chicken'. *PN Review 238* 44, 2 (December 2017).

Levin, Gabriel. 'Reading Gilgamesh'. In *Ostraca*. London: Anvil Press, 1999.

Rilke, Rainer Maria. *Briefe in zwei Bänden*. Frankfurt am Main and Leipzig: Insel Verlag, 1991.

Schrott, Raoul. *Homers Heimat: Der Kampf um Troja und seine realen Hintergründe*. Frankfurt: Hanser Verlag, 2008.

Supple, Tim. 'Ted Hughes and the Theatre'. http://ann.skea.com
/TimSupple.html.

Wisnom, Selena. 'The Journey towards Death: The Cedar Forest in
Gilgameš and Descriptions of the Netherworld'. Paper delivered in
Oxford, 2017, provided by the author.

Zukofsky, Louis. *"A"*. New York: New Directions, 1978.

Index